THE REGENCY AND VICTORIAN CRAFTS

Oval Picture of Wax Flowers.
Victoria and Albert Museum, CROWN COPYRIGHT.

THE REGENCY AND VICTORIAN CRAFTS

or

The Genteel Female - Her Arts and Pursuits

Jane Toller

WARD LOCK LIMITED
London and Sydney

ACKNOWLEDGEMENTS

The author's special thanks are due to the Eton Branch of the Buckinghamshire County Library, for their never-failing interest and co-operation in obtaining special reference books; to Mr. John Collins, for the extract from *The Universal Magazine* (Nov. 1752), used in the chapter on Paper Work; to Miss Tudor, of 'a La Ronde', Exmouth, for her kindness and courtesy; and to Miss Sheila Biggane, for the many ways in which she has helped with research.

The author and publisher would like to thank the following for allowing them to use photographs which belong to them:

H. Trevilion Esq., Plates 1A and 1B; Messrs. Mallet, Ltd., Plates 2, 17; Victoria and Albert Museum, Frontispiece and Plates 3, 12, 26; Henry Francis du Pont Winterthur Museum, Plates 4A and 4B and Plate 10; Miss Tudor, Exmouth, Plates 5, 16 and 25; Peterborough Museum, Plate 8; Miss C. Dunbar, Plate 6; National Portrait Gallery, Plate 9; Lady Lever Art Gallery, Plate 13. Plates 11, 14, 15, 18, 19, 20, 21, 22, 23, and 24 show objects in the author's collection or former collection.

The photographs in Plate 5 and 16 were taken by Messrs. Hill's Studios Exmouth. The photographs in Plates 6, 18, 19, 20, 22, 23, 24 and that on the Jacket Cover were taken by Messrs Hills and Saunders, Eton. The objects shown on the jacket cover comprise: Coat of Arms in Cut Vellum-work; Bird in Feather-work; Shell-work Cabinet; Silver-sequinned lace (Drizzling); Regency Purse (Netting or Knitting); Spectacle Case and Pin Cushion in Moose-hair Work; Unmade-up Slipper in Wool-work.

Designed by Bruce Thomas

7063 1056 x

Printed in Great Britain by Richard Clay (The Chaucer Press) Ltd Bungay, Suffolk

CONTENTS

INTRODUCTION

There has been lately a renewed interest in the sparetime occupations of our ancestresses. For some time it had been thought necessary rather to laugh at their efforts as pathetic and time-wasting – "The poor things had nothing better to do with their time," was the kind of remark one heard, said patronisingly about some unusual piece of handiwork. Then suddenly, something – was it perhaps the prices that these 'time-wasters' were fetching at auction? – aroused the interest of the female community, and female interest once aroused is not quickly or easily damped down. The result has been a revival of the crafts of our grandmothers. Words such as 'decoupage' and 'collage' have been brought back into use. Instructions appear once more in women's magazines on such things as shell-work, paper-work, feather-work and decorated furniture. I think we now need to prove to ourselves that our fingers are as nimble and our minds at least as inventive as those belonging to bygone generations of the distaff side. Yet – with one or two notable exceptions our efforts – even with modern tools and methods, appear rather stilted when compared with some of the articles illustrated in this book.

I have entertained myself for many months by doing some delightfully rewarding research into how a great many of these 'occupations' of long ago were carried out. Excluding from my list those of a more ordinary nature, I have concentrated on those that had a mystique about them. The more I have delved, the more astonished I have been at the patience, ingenuity and diligence shown by these over-derided females.

Consider the extraordinary perseverance shown by the 17th-century French Canadian nuns for instance, in their endeavours to adapt horse-hair as a substitute for embroidery silk when they became too poor to import such things from France for the making of vestments.

If sometimes I have been led a little astray down tempting by-roads, I must ask you to forgive me. I could not bear to exclude the centuries old slum-children's 'grottos' from my chapter on shell-work – or the macabre story of the Buckie House at Anstruther – though neither could really be classed as the work of "Genteel Females"!

The reader will note that fashion has always played a part in dictating the proper form that female accomplishments should take. What 18th century Mrs. Delany and her friend, the Duchess of Portland, thought of as proper things to make in their spare time, mid-19th century ladies, under the august influence of Albert the Good, despised as being frivolous. It was deemed far better to make calico shirts for the bodies of the 'heathen', and wool-work slippers for the feet of the curates. Thirty years later 'beautifying the home' was their object in making poker-work texts and macramé anti-macassars. And dare I mention this? Even in the 20th century decorating vases with Barbola-work, and pen-painting gauze table-mats were considered highly suitable leisure-hour occupations. We have now come full circle once again, and fully agree with the ideas of dear Mrs. Delany. But alas! many of us now have no space in our gardens for the erection of grottos – some of us in fact have no gardens at all. This did not in the least deter a dearly loved member of my family. Nothing daunted, and with an ingenuity Mrs. D. would herself have applauded, she made an indoor garden in a large carboy which contained a miniature grotto equally as fascinating as anything ever devised by the genteel female of long ago.

1 SHELL-WORK

Not so very long ago it was possible to buy from the seaside resorts round Britain, souvenirs in the shape of small articles covered with shells presumably picked up from that particular part of the coast. These articles were usually shell-covered miniature shoes, mirrors in shell frames or small boxes. The boxes were very popular. Very often in the middle of the lid was a picture of the resort itself – the chain-pier at Brighton for instance – and the rest of the top, and the sides of the box, were covered with shells. The box itself being lined with a bright blue glossy paper. As a child I had one of these boxes in which I kept a hoard of ribbons off chocolate boxes. The larger shells kept on getting knocked off, but this did not worry me, as I had a store of shells I had collected myself. I just selected an appropriate one and stuck it on in the vacant place.

The east coast, where we usually went for our summer holidays, had a very sandy beach. I used to walk along it after the tide had gone out searching for shells. There were tiny ones like babies' finger-nails, pairs of shells like angels' wings, razor-like shells, cockle and mussel shells, and little shiny shells called periwinkles. I loved collecting them; with what purposes in mind I do not know, for I never did anything constructive with them – except to make necklaces of the periwinkles – they just fascinated me. It was not until I became antique-minded, and started haunting museums, that I discovered that I had shared a fashion with the ladies of the 18th and early 19th centuries, in collecting shells; and was fascinated to find that they housed their collections in cabinets fitted with little drawers to take the different sized shells. Possibly some of these cabinets were made to order by the village carpenter. But the one illustrated in Plates 1A and 1B is an ornate Sheraton standing-cabinet made with drawers containing different-shaped compartments to hold larger and smaller shells which it still contains.

Plates 1 A and 1 B

On the facing page and this one is shown a Sheraton period Standing-Cabinet in mahogany, specially made to hold shells.

Later on I became interested in the kind of mother-of-pearl work used in conjunction with wood or papier-mâché. Here, of course, the shells are not used entire, but cut into various shapes to conform with the decoration used – often *chinoiserie*; and a very difficult and exacting work this cutting was.

In 1947 my husband and I bought a fascinating shell model in a glass case of 'The Garden of Paradise'. This title was on a very rubbed blue label on the back, together with the information that it had been made by two English ladies towards the end of the 18th century – I forget the exact date. Had it not been for this label we might have thought it was a production from one of the Mediterranean seaboard towns, where quite a lot of shell models were made. It was a naïve but very amusing work complete with Adam and Eve, the apple tree with entwined serpent, and various animals lurking in the bushes – all entirely composed of appropriately coloured shells. It measured about 18 inches × 12 inches and was about 12 inches high.

From collecting shells to doing something artistic with them was a natural step taken up with much fervour by the 18th-century ladies. This shell-work can be roughly divided into three categories:

1 Shell ornamentation
2 Shell pictures and models
3 Grottos and 'Gothick' cells.

Shell ornamentation

One of its most famous exponents was Mary Delany, *née* Granville, a remarkable woman by any standard. As not only this chapter, but the one on 'paper-work' contains many references to her work, a short biography might be of interest here.

She was born in 1700 of noble but impecunious parents, and at eight years of age was adopted by her aunt and uncle, Lord and Lady Stanley. They married her off much against her will, at the tender age of sixteen, to a man of over sixty. This unhappy marriage lasted for seven years, when her husband died. For the next sixteen years she lived a happy life as a widow, steadfastly refusing all offers of marriage during this time. She became a great friend of the Duchess of Portland, and was a frequent visitor at Bulstrode Park near Gerrard's Cross, Buckinghamshire, the family seat of the Portlands. (This house has now been pulled down.) In 1743 she married Dr. Daniel Delany who became Dean of Down in Ireland. They had a villa called 'Delville' near Dublin and spent most summers there, returning to England for various visits in the winter. This marriage lasted for twenty-five years and was extremely happy. After her husband's death she lived in St. James's Place, London, and was often at Bulstrode with the Duchess of Portland, who took her to the Court at Windsor where she became a firm favourite with the Royal Family. In 1785 George III presented her with a house at Windsor and a pension of £300 a year which, to add an amusing touch, was brought to her every six months in a pocket-book by Queen Charlotte, "that it might escape the tax-collector!" She died in 1788, a much beloved and revered figure, and was buried in St. James's Church, Piccadilly.

The first reference to shells I can find in her letters is in 1734 when she wrote to her sister: "I have got a new madness, I am running wild after shells. This morning I have set my little collection of shells in nice order in my cabinet, and they look so lovely that I must by some means enlarge my stock; the beauties of shells are as infinite as flowers. . . ."

She enlarged her stock by searching for them on the beaches whenever she was near the sea. The shores round Dublin must have been a very good source of supply. When she was unable to find sea-shells, she was content to search for snail-shells. There seem to have been a quantity of these at Bulstrode Park. (Snails were used medicinally a good deal at this time, so I suppose shells were readily available.)

In 1746 when she was installed at Delville she decorated a chandelier in the drawing-room in an original and pretty way with shells. Unfortunately, the house was very damp and if it was shut up for any length of time the shells would drop off.

In 1757, while she was staying at Bulstrode Park, she made four frames of shells in their natural colours, two for drawings she had done herself for the Duchess of Portland, and two for pictures worked in stones by the Duchess herself. (One was a bunch of barberries worked in amber, the other a wheat-ear, the beards of which were formed of tortoiseshell.)

In 1760 she was back at Delville again decorating with shells a room in the house which was used as a chapel. "D.D. [her husband] employs me every hour of the day for his chapel. I make the flowers and other ornaments by candle-light; and by daylight put together the festoons that are for the ceiling." This decoration was in imitation of what was then called 'stucco' – we should call it plaster-work. She had actually started making the flowers in 1750, and by the end of that year had made 86 large flowers and 30 small ones. This enormous project would appear to have been finished in 1760 for she writes: "my chief works have been the ceiling of the chapel done with cards and shells in imitation of stucco; in the chancel are four Gothick arches, two on each side made also of shells in imitation of stucco. The arches are no deeper than the thickness of the shells, to take the plain look the walls would have without them. The wreath round the window is composed of oak branches, and vines made of cards; the grapes – nuts and periwinkles; the corn – real wheat painted; all to look like stucco." (The cards she mentions were paste-board.)

An early 18th-century recipe for "*An excellent stucco, which will adhere to wood-work,*" might be of interest here:

> "Take a bushel of the best stone-lime, a pound of yellow oker, and a quarter of a pound of brown amber, all in fine powder. Mix them with a quantity of hot (not boiling) water, to a proper thickness, and lay it on with a white-washer's brush, which should be new."

May not something of this sort have been used as a foundation for the chapel ornaments?

It is a remarkable thing that such a seemingly fragile form of decoration should have survived for so long. When

H. Brimley Johnson's book *Mrs. Delany at Court and among the Wits* was published in 1925, her 'shell cornice' was still in place, a photograph was taken of it at the time, and used as an illustration to the book. This house has now been pulled down.

It would be nice to know what method was adopted of affixing these shell decorations to the walls and ceiling of the chapel. Did Mrs. Delany employ others to do the work under her direction? Someone must have helped her in any case, and what anxious hours must have been spent in getting everything into place undamaged.

In giving some advice to her sister as to how to make flounces of flowers for her dressing-table, she suggests doing the work on a frame (evidently a large tambour frame) and mounting the flowers between two fine pieces of cat-gut. She also suggests the use of starch for sticking purposes, as she finds it "better than gum". Unfortunately, there is no indication given as to what material the flowers were made of.

Shell pictures

I can find no mention of Mary Delany making shell *pictures*, though she did make 'shell-nosegays', and I have recently seen one of these shell-nosegays (which are extremely rare) enshrined in a very beautiful gilded box-frame. The nosegay itself must be about 12 inches long and 8 inches across at its broadest part. It consists of about twenty-five flowers all made of natural coloured shells. These are roses, daisies, sweet Williams, sweet-peas and pom-pom dahlias. Each petal is composed of a single shell, consequently an enormous number of shells has gone into the work. The leaves, which are few, as well as the stalks, have been carefully fashioned from some material now hard to identify. The clustered flowers, such as sweet Williams, etc., look as though each flower-head had been fixed on to separate fine brass wire, the whole bunch of wires being then incorporated in the stalk. A true lover's-knot holds the flowers in place, made of stiffened blue silk ribbon on which tiny shell flowers are 'embroidered'. The whole effect is enchanting – as can be seen from the illustration (Plate 2), which should be examined through a magnifying-glass. I could find out no history about this nosegay (or the companion one made of feathers).* There was no record about it having come from any particular house or neighbourhood; but it has obviously been made by a highly skilled artist – and the period – about the middle of the 18th century, makes it not unreasonable to suppose that it might very possibly be the work of Mrs. Delany herself. She was an expert in drawing and oil-painting, and a book of her Irish sketches is preserved in the library of one of our national museums.

The making of shell pictures, however, was a most fashionable pursuit at this time, all genteel females, from the royal princesses down, were doing it. Those who had never collected a shell in their lives could now buy them all ready collected for them at shops in fashionable quarters. The astonishing thing is that with so much done, there is so little left now.

Shell-work was popular at this time on both sides of the Atlantic in various forms – but somewhat later in the 19th century a form of shell-work known as 'Sailor's Valentines' appeared. These were composed of two frames containing shells hinged together so that they formed a box which could be closed; the shells were arranged in a formal flat method and many included a heart, or loving motto worked with the shells in the middle of the pattern. At first they were thought to be the work of sailors themselves made during their long voyages and taken home as gifts to their loved ones. But on further consideration it was felt that the operations involved were too complicated for even the handiest sailor to accomplish.

There have been through the ages many objects made by sailors, and they are always simple in origin. Scrimshaw, wooden love-tokens, snuff-boxes either of horn or wood, carved bone or wood 'sail-maker's liners', are examples, and bearing this fact in mind I agree that these 'Sailor's Valentines' were far more likely to have been ready-made presents for the seafarers to take home as keepsakes. Evidence for this

* *See chapter on 'feather-work'.*

Plate 2
Nosegay made entirely of shells. Mid-18th cent.

Plate 3

Sailor's Shell Valentine. Circa 1830.

Victoria and Albert Museum

theory seems to be to be overwhelming. All of the thirty-five different types of shells used in these Valentines were native to the West Indies. The wood used is always the same – Spanish cedar – and the construction of the boxes always the same, pointing to the one main source of supply now generally accepted as Barbados. A few even bear the motto "A present from Barbados," and none has yet appeared as a present from anywhere else.

Barbados was a shipping centre for sailing ships in the 18th and 19th centuries, and was used by American, Dutch and English ships. A box exists that actually bears the label of a Barbadian dealer, and in another a piece of crumpled newspaper (used as a base for the shells in each compartment) was found to be part of a copy of *The Barbadian* for May 15th, 1833.

Specimens of these Sailor's Valentines have been brought to England from time to time – chiefly to the western ports, but one does not often find them. Perhaps they had a greater appeal for the American sailor than for the British tar who seems to have been more attracted by the idea of a glass rolling-pin as a gift for his lady-love. (After all it was a handy way of smuggling in "Brandy for the Parson".) The Sailor's Valentine pictured in Plate 3 was presented to the Victoria and Albert Museum by Queen Mary.

Shell-dressed dolls

Objects such as birds, animals and people were made out of shells at this time. (They are still being so made in seaside places as attractions for the tourist trade.) But by far the most attractive were the wooden or composition dolls of the 18th and early 19th centuries which were dressed in clothes almost entirely made of shells, very cleverly worked in order to simulate both the material and trimmings. I know of one such doll dressed as a gentleman of the late 18th century, in a suit of blue-corded silk, embroidered with tiny shells. The shells look like raised white needlework, until closely examined. The doll is preserved under a glass dome, otherwise it would not be in such an immaculate condition.

There are two shell-dressed dolls in the Shell Museum near Holt in Norfolk; and the two pictured in Plates 4A and 4B, although English, are in the Henry Frances du Pont Winterthur Museum, Delaware.

It can be seen from these photographs how cleverly the shells have been applied to their material base to give such an interesting and fascinating effect. The shells used are common British shells, and the trays of food the maids are carrying are embellished with seaweed, to represent either salad, or fruit leaves. The dolls themselves are the typical wooden dolls, with enamelled faces, of the early 19th century.

Plates 4A and 4B
Wooden Dolls dressed entirely in shells. English, early 19th cent.

Seaweed work

Plate 5

Collage picture in Seaweed and Sand. Worked by a member of the Parminter Family, late 18th cent.

Seaweed and Sandwork

I think it proper to include in this chapter pictures made of seaweed and sand. Most of them admittedly are mid-19th century, but there are earlier examples. One of the most astounding in treatment was made, I would imagine, in the late 18th century by the Misses Parminter of Exmouth, and can still be seen in the house 'à la Ronde'. It is so thoroughly modern in treatment that it could be called a 'collage'.

The picture, Plate 5, depicts in water colour a distant view of a large 18th-century house with a castellated wing on one end. There is a solitary tree on the left in front, and an avenue of trees leading up to the house on the right of the drive. The trunks of all these trees are made of different coloured strips of seaweed, and the extremely natural-looking foliage of both these trees and the bushes in the foreground are of other types and shades of seaweed. The ground-work is made of sanded paper, which is painted in the appropriate colours of the grass, drive, etc. The sky is blue-washed watercolour and the whole is in the original wood and gesso frame. Seaweed pictures treated in this naturalistic manner must be extremely rare; there are two others at 'à la Ronde', but this is by far the most attractive. I have never seen any others of this kind.

About 1830, pictures such as the one in Plate 6 were made of baskets of variegated seaweed, including an odd shell or two, mounted on paper and framed in maple frames with gold mounts. They are much more attractive than pressed seaweed pictures, as each type stands out and looks almost as natural as it must have looked when growing. The various colours are wonderfully preserved. The picture is quite small, and amusing as well as decorative.

About thirty years later another type of seaweed picture emerged. It took the form of a print of a seaside town (not coloured) round which a wreath of different sorts of seaweed was placed. Underneath this one occasionally finds descriptive verses, and the frame is in maple. These pictures suggest that they were made by children on holiday as a wet day amusement; they cannot be compared with the earlier ones.

At this time also sand pictures were being made by the

Plate 6
Picture of arranged Seaweed in basket. Circa 1830.

ladies who lived within reasonable distance of Alum Bay in the Isle of Wight, the home of very fine sand of varying colours. They were usually very small pictures of local views, the appropriate coloured sand being stuck on, by some method, to the drawing. It was not an easy accomplishment or so I was told by an old lady who made them as a girl. (She was born about 1850.) She had two of these pictures, very beautifully done, and framed in the ubiquitous maple. One was of Winchester Cathedral, and the other of Saint Cross near Winchester. But she would not tell me how they were made, though I tried very hard to find out.

I suppose the taste for sand pictures was started by Benjamin Zobel – an artist who was responsible for the decoration of the dining-tables at Windsor Castle during the Regency period. He made sand pictures down the middle of these for banquets. It is said that he was so upset to see all his hard work swept away that he invented a method whereby the sand would stick permanently. Whether he applied this method to his table decoration I do not know, but I have seen six fairly large pictures by him, all of animals (rather after the Morland School) grazing in Windsor Park. He very cleverly raised the ground-work in some way, so that various features stood out, rather like stump-work in embroidery. In some lights his pictures look like ordinary watercolours, but in other lights the sand glistens, giving a rather delightful effect.

Whether efforts by amateurs, or professionally done by Zobel, sand pictures are rare.

Grottos

In the third category, 'Gothick Cells' or 'Grottos' were all the rage in the 18th and early 19th centuries in Britain.

Formal gardens were things of the past; the emphasis now was on landscaped gardens with vistas or groves; at the end of which were Gothick Cells, or grottos to which an air of mystery was imparted by the shrubberies which surrounded them. If the garden included a lake with an island, then this was the obvious place for such a work of art.

Minerals – quartzes, marbles and fossils – were the favourite materials in use, but shells were often added. This was essentially a mistake because they could not always survive the vagaries of the climate, and they did not look their best out of doors away from their natural environment.

Mary Delany has quite a lot to say about grottos. One, which she visited near Dublin in 1732, was decorated with shells "in a variety of patterns; pink shell, pearly shell, blue shell, white shell, cleverly imbedded in the dark olive green of the wall."

Another Irish grotto was that of the Bishop of Killala, which was also decorated with shells collected from the beach by members of his house party, which included John Wesley and Mary Delany herself.

In 1756 while staying in Bristol she visited a grotto made

by Mr. Golding, the Quaker, which was then not much more than half finished. She describes it thus: "Four pillars support a dome with a skylight, on the left hand in perspective one arch within another; there is a statue of a river god; a cascade falls from thence over rocks, coral, shells, and is received into a bason. The pillars are covered with spars of this country. . . . It is much the finest thing of the kind I ever saw; though I could not but grudge at the shells *sacrificed there*, and exposed to the ruin of damp and time, that would have preserved their beauty for ages in a cabinet!"

She also helped the Duchess of Portland and her daughters to make a Gothick Cell in the grounds at Bulstrode which "was as beautiful and elegant as amber, ivory, jet, and mother-of-pearl could make it." (She obviously did not object to the use of mother-of-pearl.)

There were many other notable grottos – Pope's grotto at Twickenham; that of Lord Shaftesbury at Wimborne St. Giles in Dorset, which was made of imported shells, and cost over £10,000; the famous Grotto Hall of Woburn, (which strictly speaking is not a grotto at all, but a shell-decorated room), and many others. But we are not concerned so much with these professionally made ones as with those made by the ladies of the house, of which there must have been many all over the country. It was by no means only the nobility that was interested in such matters. Many years ago I visited an uncle who had an old house on the borders of Bedfordshire and Buckinghamshire. He was fortunate enough to have two grottos in his grounds. One was, in a way, more of a summer-house than a grotto, in that it had two windows. It was hexagonal in shape, and the walls were covered with pebbles. Opposite the door, on the back wall, were two or three mock windows made of looking-glass and framed in shells. The other grotto was a round building rather like a Rockingham cottage, in the corner of what once had been a herb-garden (now given over more prosaically to vegetables). The inside walls were completely covered in shells done in variegated patterns, there were pointed Gothic windows and the roof was thatched. The ladies of the house were probably inspired to such efforts by the Grotto Hall at Woburn Abbey – which was not far away. The house itself was indisputably haunted by a young man who had been treacherously murdered there by a friend. Luckily the haunting did not extend to the grounds.

So we have grottos professionally and expensively made at the behest of rich men in their parks; grottos built to pass the time away by energetic females in gardens; and there are the humbler grottos made by the children through many centuries in the meaner streets of London, for I feel I cannot let this chapter end without mentioning the absorbingly interesting story of the shell-work grottos that have survived every kind of calamity, including two of the worst wars in history.

London children in the Middle Ages saw many pilgrims depart to the shrine of St. James at Compostella. They saw them return with the scallop or cockle-shell – a sign they had made the pilgrimage – fastened to their cloaks and hats. They must have heard of the miraculous burial of this saint in a sepulchre or grotto at Compostella, that was afterwards glorified by a shrine. Being insular-minded they saw no reason why they should not have their own grottos. People unable to go on the pilgrimage might like to see a shrine to the saint near at hand. If scallop or cockle-shells were not always obtainable, at the time of the feast of St. James (July 25th), oysters were coming into season. They were cheap and plentiful, and not – as they are now – a rich man's dish. There were plenty of empty shells to be found in the open drains outside the taverns. The children collected these, and made grottos of them; cone-like edifices made of layers and layers of oyster-shells, with an entrance in the base. At the top they put a rush-light or tallow-dip. These 'votive candles' would not have lasted very long, and it may have been that the passers-by threw them pennies to provide others. Hence the cry of "Please remember the Grotto!"

After the Reformation people who had never heard of pilgrimages to Compostella still connected oysters with St. James's day and a proverb sprang up: "He who eats oysters on St. James's day will not lack for money."

London children were still making grottos of oyster-shells in Victorian days (Plate 7) but later on the supply of shells began to dwindle – not so much due to the fact that oysters were becoming more expensive, but rather that there were no more open drains; only dust-bins in enclosed back-yards, where they dared not go. So the grottos were made of heaps of sand or earth, decorated with shells, and no longer supplied with candles, but the cry "A penny for the Grotto" still continued.

Plate 7
Victorian Street Grotto of Oyster-shells. Chambers' 'Book of Days'.

I have seen many of these grottos myself. In some of the very poverty-stricken streets before the war, they were made of cardboard boxes with pitiful tufts of grass for decoration – but however poverty-stricken, and despite what was happening in the outside world, grottos still persisted. For five years whole areas of London slums were laid waste by bombs, but the idea of grotto-making did not die out, for when the war was over, orthodox grottos appeared once again. In 1954 a 12-year-old Camberwell boy wrote this description of a grotto made by a group of his schoolfellows: "First a big pile of sand and earth was put on a board about 3 feet × 2 feet. Then tunnels were burrowed into it. When the tunnels were finished pieces of coloured china were stuck in the walls. Small rock-like stones were placed in it. In some places a small tin lid was filled with water, these were embedded in the tunnels also. Around the outside, pieces of moss and glass covered the earth and sand, and were studded with flowers."

Broken bits of coloured china here take the place of shells, probably not now so easy to obtain around Camberwell – but otherwise this description of the grotto bears a fantastic resemblance to those erected in the 18th century. Camberwell is a densely built-up working-class area, and a grotto such as this could not have been erected on its busy pavements but was built instead on a *bomb site* (many such places being favourite play-grounds for years after the war). Naturally all the materials used would be to hand – even to the flowers – which seemed to flourish miraculously in such places.

Perhaps the most macabre grotto is at Buckie House, Anstruther, Scotland (Buckie is a Fife word for shell). The whole of the outside of the front of the house, and half-way up the side, is decorated with buckies. This was done by a Mr. Batchelor who lived there over a hundred years ago. Inside the house was a room known as the Grotto, the ceiling of which was decorated elaborately with shells. Inside this room he kept his coffin, which was also decorated with shells. Visitors had to pay to view the grotto, and for an extra charge Mr. Batchelor would climb inside the coffin and close the lid on himself!

2 PAPER-WORK

Flower pictures

Curiously enough the finest picture of this kind I have seen was not made by an English lady of leisure, but by a French prisoner-of-war who was incarcerated at Norman Cross Prison near Peterborough. This picture is now in the Peterborough Museum (Plate 8). The flowers have been cut either from ordinary drawing paper, and afterwards varnished with a clear varnish to stiffen and preserve them, or from parchment, which is stiff enough not to need this treatment. At any rate this is a beautiful and delicate piece of work, done on a coloured background and framed in a box-frame.

The very few others I have seen have been, compared with this, very amateurish affairs, with not much shape to the flowers, and of no artistic merit. Obviously this particular branch of paper-work was a difficult and exacting task, needing an artist's eyes and perception.

Mrs. Delany, at the advanced age of 72, invented a new form of cut-paper work which she described as 'paper mosaicks', and she had completed nearly 1,000 of these pictures before her eyesight failed ten years later. Her collection was named by her the 'Flora Delanica', and one of the last pictures to be added to it was a study of a Jamaican shrub named after the Duchess of Portland. This particular 'mosaick' was based on a specimen forwarded to her from the Royal Botanical Gardens at Kew. We are told that the "King and Queen always desired that any curious or beautiful plant should be transmitted to Mrs. Delany when in blossom."

Plate 8

Flower Picture in Cut-paper Work.

The idea for these paper mosaicks came to this lady quite suddenly one day when she was idly playing with a piece of scarlet paper – the episode is described thus in the introduction written by Brimley Johnson to *Mrs. Delany*:

"Having a piece of Chinese paper on the table of bright scarlet, a geranium caught her eye of a similar colour, and taking her scissors she amused herself with cutting out each flower by her eye in the paper which resembled its hue. She laid the paper petals on a black ground, and was so pleased with the effect that she proceeded to cut out the calyx, stalks and leaves in shades of green, and pasted them down; after she had completed a sprig of geranium in this way, the Duchess of Portland came in and exclaimed 'What are you doing with the geranium?' – having taken the paper imitation for the real flower – Mrs. Delany answered that if the Duchess 'really thought that it so like the original, a new work was begun from that moment'."

This new work was done in the following manner:

"She placed the growing plant before her with a background of black paper doubled in the form of a folding screen. This dark background threw out distinct outlines of the leaves and flowers. Then, using as a base a sheet of drawing-paper washed over with Indian ink to make it a dull black, she cut out *by eye*, and laid on each flower or petal as it appeared. The lights and shades and tints were also laid on, being pasted one over the other.

"The stamens, styles and leaves were separately done in various coloured papers which she used to procure from 'Captains of vessels coming from China', or from 'paper-stainers'; from whom she used to buy pieces of paper in which the colours had run and produced extraordinary and unusual tints. In this manner she was able to produce the utmost brilliancy where it was required, with the greatest harmony of colouring for the various semi-tones of tints laid on. Every part necessary to complete the outline and shading of every leaf, flower and stem was cut

Plate 9
Mary Delany by J. Opie (about the time she was making her Paper-Mosaicks).
National Portrait Gallery, London.

out without a fault in perspective, or in the most difficult foreshortening."

As Mrs. Delany was an accomplished artist, perspective and foreshortening might not have presented many difficulties to her, and she had been used to snipping birds and flowers out of paper before she was ten years old. Nevertheless she produced things of great beauty and artistry, at which we can well marvel.

The Royal Family were so much interested in her work that she offered "with the utmost fearfulness of being too presumptious, as a lowly tribute of her humble duty and earnest gratitude," several of her pictures to Queen Charlotte.

Paper-filigree

Paper-filigree simulating gold filigree, enriched with beads and gold threads was used in English ecclesiastical art during the 15th century up to the time of the Reformation. The art was again revived – this time in a secular way – from 1660–1715, when the materials included seed pearls, small shells and metal threads; and incorporated painted miniatures, carved cameos, wax portraits and figures. Many examples at this time were in the form of framed and glazed panels used as wall decoration. In the Lady Lever Art Gallery, Port Sunlight, there is a portrait of Queen Anne in wax and paper-filigree, *circa* 1710. This is a magnificent piece of work containing a great deal of the rolled-paper work that was to come much more into prominence at a later date. Also in the Lady Lever Art Gallery is a portrait bust of a child in wax, with an intensely ornate surround of paper-filigree. It is signed with a monogram and dated 1702.

At a slightly later date rolled-paper work combined with other materials was being done in America; it seems to have originated in New England, especially round about Boston, and was termed 'quill-work'. This name is slightly puzzling, as quill-work generally is the term applied to the embroidery on the moccasins, pouches, etc of the North American Indian tribes, which was done with animal hairs and small portions of porcupine quills. (See chapter on 'hair-work'.)

Rolled-paper quill-work was used, like the English quill-work at the beginning of the century, to form decorative panels; in this case in the form of candle-sconces. The work was framed in glazed box-frames – much the same shape as Queen Anne mirrors – made of moulded wood painted black, or gilded. In some cases the frame had a carved 'crest'. The candle sconce illustrated in Plate 10 is presumed to be the work of Elizabeth Hunt, the daughter of John Hunt, a wealthy merchant of Boston. (The silver candle arms were made by the Boston Silversmith (1702–1758) and stamped with the die he used between 1729–40.)

Quill-work does not consist by any means entirely of paper; many other interesting materials were used such as wax, shells, ground pine, barberries, spines of feathers, silk fibre and gilt beads. The backgrounds had mica or ground glass scattered over glue to give a sparkle to the work.

The designs in quill-work were much freer than those in paper-filigree, and the whole effect much less stylised. Luckily many of them have been carefully preserved, and can be seen in several American museums. A decorative panel at the Essex Institute, Salem, is considered to be European and not American. It is very similar in design and execution to that in the Lady Lever Art Gallery, but in the place of the wax bust there is a small oval painting of the Madonna and Child.

Most of this American work is authenticated, the name of the artist and the date being known. Daughters from well-to-do families went to special schools where the whole process of quill-work was taught; and the necessary materials supplied, including the frames, which probably were supplied with the mica background already in place ready to be worked on.

Paintings were expensive at this time, and mirrors probably the only method of decorating the walls; so these works of art were no doubt treasured almost as much for their decorative value, as for the display of talent shown by the daughters of the house – and how proudly this must have been displayed!

At the time that quill-work was fashionable in America,

Plate 10
One of a pair of Candle-sconces in Quill-work. American. Circa 1730.

paper-filigree had quite gone out of favour in England, and did not return till the 1760–1770s, when it was revived mainly as the art of ladies of leisure. The form had now changed – the style also – being now flatter, and much more concentrated. The craze was now for hatchments, coats-of-arms, and other small decorative panels carried out entirely in paper or vellum, and framed in 'Hogarth' box-frames with bright blue paper backgrounds.

The vogue for this kind of work I feel sure must have been started by a very expert professional exponent, one Nathaniel Bermingham who, according to *Mortimer's Universal Directory* of 1763 was a "Herald Painter, and improver of a curious art of cutting out Portraits and Coats-of-Arms in vellum, with the aid of a penknife. Several specimens of this his peculiar talent may be seen at his house, at the corner of Queen Street and Long Acre." One of the 'specimens' was a picture of Britannia holding a portrait of Frederick, Prince of Wales. Bermingham's 'curious art' became very popular with the nobility and gentry, and specimens of his meticulous work occasionally come on to the market today.

The coat-of-arms illustrated in Plate 11 may have been his work. It represents the arms of the Northcotes, and came into the possession of my husband's family through the marriage of Mary Northcote to John Toller in the mid-18th century. The Northcotes at that time had no male heir, and the men who married the daughters were requested to add the name of Northcote to their own surname. It is an unbelievably fine piece of work in cut vellum on a blue background. The crosses on the right of the shield are painted black, and the one on the left is red. It is in its original frame – still practically unimpaired by time. If this were indeed the work of Mary Northcote herself she must have been a highly gifted artist. Naturally enough Bermingham's efforts were copied by amateurs, and patterns were sold specially for them. The *New Lady's Magazine* for 1786 issued a series of twelve sheets of patterns and some sixty motifs in all. These were designed by the engraver Styart. Other professionals had taken up the work, however, and a Mrs. Rigg exhibited two

Plate 11
Coat-of-Arms in Cut Vellum.
Mid-18th cent.

pieces of cut-paper at the Free Society of Artists in 1764, and a Mrs. Seymour exhibited several items there in 1765–6, including 'a head of the King of Poland', cut in vellum, a 'landscape', a 'squirrel with a nut-bough'; coats-of-arms and cyphers.

Rolled-paper work

This was a popular form of decorating coasters, boxes or tea-caddies, and was done in this manner: a stiff paper or parchment was cut into strips about an eighth of an inch wide; sometimes the edges were gilded, sometimes tinted a red colour. These strips were then folded into shapes of leaves, swags, etc. and glued on to the article to be decorated, which had been covered with tinfoil or other decorative paper, sometimes even with thin mirror glass. The interstices left between these decorations were then filled in with tightly rolled strips of paper stuck on as close together as possible. (See Plate 12.) Sometimes the main piece of decoration was a miniature painting with a frame of paper leaves or plaits. Sometimes the whole of the work was gilded and burnished to give the effect of real gold filigree.

The period when this work was being done was largely influenced by the work of Sheraton, and the shape of the tea-caddies is always Sheraton in style, either oval or hexagonal. The boxes were specially made by the cabinet-makers, and had shallow depressions in each panel to take the paper-work; the lid was rimmed with hardwood of some sort, box-wood, ebony, etc. Charles Elliot, a cabinet-maker who was purveyor of furniture to George III, supplied one to Princess Elizabeth. It had an ebony moulding, lock and key, and was lined inside and out. He also supplied with the box, fifteen ounces of different filigree papers and one ounce of gold paper.

A few words about Charles Elliott, 1753–1832, might not be amiss here; as a success story his equals that of Dick Whittington. His father had been a Jacobite fugitive who, after many years abroad, returned to England where he had a post with H.M. Customs at Burnham-on-Crouch in Essex. After his death his family were left in poor circumstances, and Charles, at the age of 18, went up to London to find a job, with one shilling in his pocket. He entered the cabinet-making business and so well did he get on that in 1774 he became a partner in the firm of Davis and Elliott at 97 New Bond Street. His business flourished and in 1783, at the age of 30, he was the sole owner of the firm. The year following he received his first royal appointment. He was the only royal furniture-maker who was also employed as a general contractor and decorator, and in 1803 he was included in Sheraton's list of Master Cabinet-Makers. He died in 1832 and was then worth nearly half a million pounds. (His daughter Charlotte Elliot, an invalid, was the celebrated author of several well-known hymns.)

The *Gentleman's Magazine* for 1791 mentions that an enormous number of tea-caddies with filigree-paper panels were being decorated by young ladies, but they were also

Plate 12
Rolled-paper Tea caddy. Circa 1800.

being made by French prisoners-of-war. There is one similar to that illustrated which is known to have been done by a prisoner at the Falmouth Depot, before he was transferred to the prison at Norman Cross near Peterborough, where two others were made. This rolled-paper work would therefore seem to be French in origin as it is highly unlikely that a prisoner could have learnt the work so perfectly while languishing in gaol. The amateur work of the ladies was done on professionally made boxes, the French prisoners' work was done on boxes knocked-up from whatever material they could find for the job – which would be most likely pine; probably lined with the pink paper which was used for the straw-work boxes made at the same prison. The hinges and escutcheons on any of this prisoner-of-war work are usually very crude, being hammered out of any scraps of metal available.

Paper-filigree and rolled-paper work, as well as being used on small objects, were also used as decoration on furniture. One piece decorated in this manner – a cabinet and stand (Plate 13) – can be seen at the Lady Lever Art Gallery. It is an extremely fine piece of work; an entry from *Macquoid's Catalogue* reads as follows:

> "Cabinet and Stand, entirely covered with a decoration of small rolls of coloured paper, called at the time 'Filigree Work'. The front and sides are decorated in imitation of mosaic with birds, butterflies and flowers, in the centre of which are coloured prints after Morland, those on the outside of the doors being framed and suspended by a ribbon formed of pearl beads inserted in the rolls of paper. The panels are framed, like the cornice, in an ingenious arrangement of small ovals. The inside of the doors have panels of flowers painted on white satin, evidently by an amateur, and are further embellished with coloured glass flat beads. When open, fourteen drawers and a small cupboard are visible, all differently ornamented in the paper rolls and beads, to simulate mosaic, and exceedingly bright in colour. The legs of the stand taper slightly, and are

Plate 13

Cabinet on Stand decorated with Filigree Work, with hand-painted panels.

decorated on all four sides with diminishing husking in reds and greens on a dark ground."
English, *circa* 1778. Height on stand, 4 ft. 10 in.
Length, 2 ft. Depth, 1 ft. 5½ in.

Such pieces are extremely rare.

Another kind of cut-paper work was that which grew naturally out of the art of cutting silhouettes. Here figures of people and animals, trees, birds, horses, huntsmen, etc. were snipped out of paper and pasted on to a contrasting background. Like silhouettes, the process could be reversed, the cut-out portion discarded, and the remainder backed with a black or coloured paper. The result was something which looked as if it was made of lace, an extremely fascinating effect. Some of these little pictures are really marvellous and a magnifying-glass is needed to study them properly. One such can be seen at the house (open to the public at certain times) 'à la Ronde' at Exmouth. The process was done entirely by hand with a pair of scissors. There was a great deal of this work done by amateurs and professionals both in this country and America (where I believe the best work was done in Pennsylvania by German artists). Many amateurs folded the paper before cutting it; and this method persists to this day in remote country places as a form of shelf covering. Cut from 'lining' paper, wall-paper or newspaper, the piece needed is made about 6 or 8 inches wider than the shelf itself. The paper is then folded, and a scalloped edge cut, with other pieces snipped out here and there to make a design when unfolded. I was myself initiated into this art at an early age by one of our maids who came from Derbyshire, and we both took great pride in our papered shelves.

Among my collection of needlework tools I have a pair of scissors I am convinced were made for the very fine cut-out work. The blades are barely an inch long, and very pointed and sharp. The finger and thumb holes seem very large in comparison, but the scissors are well balanced, and comfortable to use.

Pin-prick and other paper-work

Paper seems to have been highly valued by the ladies of the 18th century, not only to cut out, and draw and paint on, but – of all unlikely materials – to embroider on. This was done in the middle of the century when superfine needles were being made. I once found one of these needles inside a

Plate 14
Fine Embroidery on Paper. 18th cent.

pin-cushion that had disintegrated, and I would not have thought anything less fine than human hair could have been threaded through the eye. But very fine embroidery silks were also being made, and the temptation to try them both out on paper must have proved too strong. One such picture is illustrated in Plate 14. The embroidery is very fine, and it appears to have been worked on ordinary writing paper.

Another one, worked on paper, which passed through our hands recently was a figure subject. The faces and hands of the boy and girl depicted in it were painted in watercolour. The clothes were of material appliquéd on with a couching stitch. The scenery in the background was also painted. The whole was in a maple frame.

In the early 19th century a craze sprung up for 'dressing' the fashion prints out of magazines. Suitable material was pasted on to the prints, and the result was rather charming.

This idea was much copied in the 1930s. Victorian fashion prints, which could be picked up quite cheaply, were 'dressed' in brightly coloured silks, satins and brocades. This was not such a very far cry from the 'tinsel' pictures of an earlier period, where prints of famous living actors, depicted in various Shakespearian rôles, were decorated with tinsel and framed in cheap black reeded frames. These prints sold at '1d plain' and '2d coloured' – hence the well-known phrase still in use.

A very unusual form of paper picture was done by a method we might call 'pin-prick'. I believe it to be of French origin and though I have seen very little of this work, luckily I have one example, which I can describe here.

The picture itself is about 14 inches long and 8 inches wide, and depicts a figure in the very simple white dress and cap of an 18th-century peasant girl.

The figure has first of all been embossed by some method on the paper, so that all the contours are raised from the surface; the face, neck, arms and hands are laid over with a flesh-coloured silk material on which the features, etc. are painted.

Each fold of the dress has been pin-pricked in a different direction, so that the lights and shades, as well as the folds of the dress, fichu and cap are emphasised. The hair and shoes are painted black. The background has been left in its plain white state, but despite this the figure stands out most effectively. At a quick glance one might think the dress is an appliqué of embroidered linen – and I suppose this is the effect the pin-pricks are meant to achieve. A combination of cut-paper and pin-prick work was done by Amelia Blackburn in the early 19th century.

Silhouettes were also cut out of black paper pasted on to a white ground, but this work, though engaged in by some amateurs, was more of a professional accomplishment. It is a subject in itself, and much has been written about it.

Paper used decoratively is still with us in the form of paper flowers, and – to the joy of young children who enjoy messing about with scissors and paste – paper-chains for Christmas decorations.

Paper flowers

From an early Victorian magazine under the heading *The Englishwoman's Corvezzione* the following remarks on paper flowers are culled:

> "We foresee the time when paper flowers will, in abundance, adorn every home that has any pretensions to taste. Two or three whole-sized plants nicely imitated, put into ordinary flower pots, and arranged amongst a few natural evergreens, may decorate nooks and niches where, for the want of sufficient light, camelias, geraniums, fuchsias etc., would refuse to flourish. Then again, branches of ivy (one of the very best subjects for the student in flower making to begin upon) may be made to festoon and depend for innumerable places – the sides of book-shelves, brackets, vases, etc.* And a not unimportant recommendation to paper flower making is, that when a petal or piece of foliage is damaged, it can easily be replaced by a new one."

Paper-ware or papier-mâché

Paper-ware, or papier-mâché, as it came to be called, was the result of an effort to find a substitute for wood that would stand up to the intense heat necessary for the baking of lacquered furniture.

When lacquer cabinets, etc., imported from China became the rage in Europe at the end of the 17th and beginning of the 18th centuries, efforts on the part of English and Dutch cabinet-makers to imitate this work were not always entirely successful. This was due to the fact that the wood used in making the objects suffered very much in the baking necessary for hardening the lacquer, the severe heat cracking or warping the wood panels.

In China the lacquered objects were dried in caves in the natural heat of the country. It may have been a long process, but it was a satisfactory one. Open-air drying was not possible in the British or Dutch climates, and anyhow a quicker process was necessary for European cabinet-makers who

* *Substitute 'plastic' for the word 'paper' and this might be a description of a certain type of modern home today!*

wished to market their goods as soon as possible. Various experiments in making a substitute material of toughened paper were then carried out, and in 1758 Robert Donne, in his book *The Handmaid of the Arts*, gave an outline of a method of making heat-resisting paper-ware. In 1765 the Rev. T. Crowther also gave details of a paper-pulp process.

Eventually, owing to an invention started by John Baskerville, the celebrated printer, of using panels made of a number of paper sheets pasted together (a process perfected by his apprentice Henry Clay in 1772), a substance was found that was so hard that it could be treated in every way like wood; it could be sawn, dove-tailed, screwed, etc. This substance became known as papier-mâché.

At first Clay experimented with coach-panels in this medium, then with trays and finally graduated to furniture. His factory was in Birmingham, and after he had been appointed 'Japanner in Ordinary to the King,'* the Birmingham Directory of 1781, referring to his work, said that "several pieces of superb furniture, which now adorn the royal residences, have been made."

This may come as a surprise to those readers who have thought of papier-mâché as a Victorian substance only suitable for the manufacture of fragile bric-à-brac; but many of the pieces Clay made between 1772 and 1812 survive, almost as good as new, to this day, and can be seen in museums and private collections.

In the meanwhile making objects of paper-pulp and lacquering them was an occupation that entertained many amateurs. They called it 'Japan-work' and in 1728 Mary Delany was writing: "Everybody is mad about 'Japan-work', I hope to be a dab at it by the time I see you." Little if any of their efforts has stood the test of time. Nevertheless, I am giving the following 18th-century recipe in full because I am sure it will be of great interest to workers in papier-mâché and lacquering both here and in America, where the latter occupation has been taken up by various ladies' guilds in a highly professional manner.

An extract from the *Universal Magazine*, 1752:

* *George III.*

A RECIPE FOR PAPER-WARE
The method of japanning wood or paper

The people of Japan have a method of making plates, bowls, and other vessels of brown paper, and sometimes of fine saw-dust.

The vessels are very light and strong after they have been varnished; the method of making them is as follows:

Boil a quantity of slips or pieces of brown paper in common water, mashing them with a stick while it is boiling, till it has almost become a paste; then take it out of the water, and pound it well in a mortar till it comes to a pumice like rags pounded in the trough of a paper-mill.

Then take gum arabic, a quantity sufficient to cover the paper paste an inch thick; put these together in a large pipkin and let them boil, stirring them very well together, till you think the paper paste is impregnated with the gum; then, having a mould ready, give the paste the form or shape you desire to put it into; the *mould* is made as follows:

As for example, suppose you design to make a thing in the form of a pewter or earthen plate, you must procure a hard piece of wood to be turned by a turner on one side of such a form (i.e. like the back of a plate,) and a hole or two made in the middle quite through the wood; and besides this, another hard piece of wood must be turned, much of the same figure, about the one-eighth part of an inch less than the former; and if you please you may have some little ornament engraved on the wood. Oil these moulds very well on the sides that are turned, continuing to oil them till they are well soaked with oil; then they are fit for use.

When you are about to make a plate of the paper paste, take that mould that has the hole in it, and having oiled it again, set it even upon a strong table, and spread over it some of your paste, as equally as possible, as to be everywhere a quarter of an inch thick. Then oil the other paper mould very well, and set it exactly as maybe on your paste, and press it hard down, then set a great weight upon it, and let it stand for twenty-four hours.

N.B. The hole at the bottom is for the water to pass through that is pressed out of the paste, and the oiling of the moulds is to prevent the gummed paste from sticking to the wood. When the paste is dry it will be as hard as a board, and be fit to lay a ground upon, made with strong size and lamp-black; then let it stand to dry. Mix ivory-black finely ground with the following varnish:

To Make the Strong Japan Varnish

Take an ounce of colophony, and having melted it in a glazed pipkin, and having ready three ounces of amber reduced to a fine powder, sprinkle it little by little into it, adding now and then some spirit of turpentine; when this is melted, sprinkle in three ounces of sarcocolla finely powdered, stirring all the while, and putting in frequently more spirit of turpentine till all is melted; then pour it through a coarse hair bag, placed between two hot boards, and press it gently till the clear is received into a warm glazed vessel.

Mix ground ivory-black with this varnish, and, having just warmed your paper plate, paint it in a warm room before the fire, as equally as you can, and set it into a gentle oven, and on the third day into one very hot, and let it stand in it till the oven is quite cold, and then it will be fit for any use, either for containing liquors cold or hot, and will never change, nor can these sorts of vessels be broke without great difficulty.

It is highly probable that if the moulds were cast of any hard metal, they might do better than wood.

The Method of Making Vessels of Sawdust

Take saw-dust, and having dried it well, pour on it some turpentine, with an equal quantity of resin, and half as much bees-wax; mix them well, and put them to your dry saw-dust stirring all together till the mixture becomes as thick as a paste; then take it off the fire, and having warmed the moulds, spread some of your mixture on that which has a hole in the middle, as equally as possibly can be, and press down the upper mould upon it, then set it by, let it stand till it is cold, and the vessel will be fit for painting.

You may, when the turpentine is melted, put in some sarcocolla, finely powdered, to the quantity of half the turpentine, stirring it well, and this will harden it. This composition ought to be made in the open air because, being apt to take fire, it will endanger the house. But whichever of the methods you make use of if you would have them look like gold, do them over with size, and when that begins to stick a little to the fingers, lay on leaf-gold. Although the leaf-gold is tender, and may be subject to rub off, yet the varnish with which it is covered, will keep it bright and entire.

After the gold has been laid on, and the gold size is dry, and the loose flying pieces brushed off, then lay in the following varnish to brighten the gold and preserve it from rubbing.

Varnish for Gold

Melt some colophony, and then put in two ounces of amber well pulverised, with some turpentine, as the amber thickens, stirring it well. Then add an ounce of gum elemi, well powdered, and some more spirit of turpentine, still keeping the liquor stirring till it is all well mixed; but take care to use as little spirit of turpentine as you can, because the thicker the varnish is, the harder will it be. Let this operation be performed over a sand-heat in an open glass, and strain it as directed for the former varnish.

Use this varnish alone, first warming your vessels made with the paper-paste, and lay it on with a painting brush before the fire, and afterwards harden it by degrees at three several times in ovens, the first being a slow heat, the next a warmer oven, and the third a very hot one, and these vessels will look like polished gold.

(The vessels that are made with saw-dust and gums, may

be varnished in the same way, with the same ingredients with the exception of the gum-elemi; and these will dry in the sun, or in a very gentle warmth.)

The Method of Silvering these Japanned Vessels

After the vessels have been made and thoroughly dried, do them over with size, or with ground chalk or whiting; let them stand by till they are very dry, and then paint them over again with the brightest gold size that you can get, (for there is a great deal of difference in the colour of it, some of it is almost white, and other yellow; the latter is proper for gold, and the former for silver.) When this size is almost dry, lay on the leaf-silver, and close it well to the size, brushing off the loose parts, when it is dry, with some cotton.

When you lay your leaf-silver keep it from the air, for the least motion of the air will rumple the leafs, and they will not lie smooth; then use the following varnish to clear the silver.

To Make the Varnish

Melt some turpentine in a fine-glazed pipkin, then take one ounce and a half of white amber well pulverised, put it in by degrees into the turpentine, stirring it well till the amber is all dissolved; then put to it half an ounce of Sarcocolla powdered, and half an ounce of gum elemi well lavigated, pouring in at times more of the turpentine-spirit till all is dissolved. Let it be done over a gentle fire, and keep stirring the mixture continually while it is on the fire.

This varnish will be as white and strong as the former, and must be warm, and is to be afterwards hardened by degrees in an oven, (the same as the gold varnish was) and the vessel will look like polished silver.

To Make Paper Vessels of a Red Colour with gilded figures on them

Mix some vermillion with the varnish first directed, and use it warm, then stove it or warm it by degrees in an oven, and it will be extremely bright.

Or else lay on the first ground with size and vermillion, and, with gum arabic water, stick on in proper places, some figures cut out of prints, as little sprigs of flowers or such-like, and, when they are dry, do them over with gold size, and let them remain till it is a little sticky to the touch, then lay on the gold, and let that be well closed to the gold size and dried.

Then, if you have a mind to shade any part of the flower, trace over the shady parts on the leaf-gold, with a fine pencil of camel-hair and some ox-gall, and then paint on that with a deep Dutch pink; and when that is dry, use the varnish in a warm place, (i.e. the varnish directed for the covering of gold), and when you have done set it to harden by degrees in an oven. This varnish will secure the leaf-gold by keeping the air from it.

Directions in Colouring Prints of Birds, Flowers, etc. in Japanning Vessels

If the prints or drawings of flowers be in black and white, if the centre of the flower is rising, you may touch the edges of the lights with a thin tincture of Gamboge, and lay in some Dutch pink, or gallstone, over the shades, so as to run into the lights a very little. This is to be done, because the thrums in the middle of flowers are generally yellow; but if of any other colour, then touch the verges of the whites with a little ultra-marine blue, and over the shades either some sanders blue, to run a little to the ultra-marine, or else a little shade with indigo; and some of the white of the print, being left void of colour, will then give life and spirit to the colours so disposed.

All flowers should be tenderly touched in the light, just to give a little glare into the light parts of the colour you would give to the flower leaves; and if you paint by a natural flower you will presently see that, on the shady side, you must lay on the most shady part, such a colour as will force the rest to appear forward; but do not daub over the shades with too heavy a colour; let it be such as may be transparent if possible, and scrumble it into the light colour that was laid before. On this occasion the pencil must be used but lightly, with a very little gum water in it, and it must be used before the colours are quite dry.

In painting the leaves of plants and herbs, regard must be had to the colour of the greens, that sometimes being the chief distinguishing character. Of greens verdigris is the lightest; therefore that colour should be touched into the lighter part of the leaf, from the place where the lighter parts of the shades end; and then in the shady parts, lay on some sap green, so as to unite with the verdigris green; and if the natural leaf should be of a darkish colour, touch the lighter sides of the leaves with a little verdigris, green, and Dutch yellow and pink mixed together, or with a tincture of French berries, but so as to leave the verdigris shine more than the pink.

The leaving the lights in colouring the prints has two advantages, viz.:

If the whites be left on this occasion, the whiteness of the paper serves instead of white paint, which is a heavy colour, and would rather confound those that have been prescribed to be laid on, than do them any service; but the colours before directed, where there is no white laid on, will shine agreeably into the white of the paper. I am the more particular in this because some persons will lay a blue flower all over with one colour, tho' it be thick enough to hide both the lights and the shades; and then it will look like a penny picture, where there is nothing but a jumble of reds, blues, and greens. In such pieces of work, be sure to scrumble the lights into the shades of every colour, and leave the middle of the lights open to the paper; for as the paper is white, of itself it makes a light.

Author's note: *This advice for painting on paper could well be adhered to when painting on mother-of-pearl inlay. Many restorations of such work have suffered from much too heavy a paint being used, so that the mother-of-pearl is quite obliterated, and there is then no reason for it having been used at all.*

3 FEATHER-WORK

In the 18th century feather-work was a fashionable occupation among young ladies on both sides of the Atlantic. An advertisement in the *Boston Gazette* dated 1755 announced that:

> "Mrs. Hiller still continues to keep school in Hanover Street, a little below the Orange Tree, where young Ladies may be taught Wax-work, Transparant and Filigree, Painting on glass, Quill-work and Featherwork, Japanning, Embroidery with silver and gold."

Unfortunately very little of this feather-work survives anywhere today, which makes a study of the subject difficult.

Perhaps it was not such a popular occupation as some of the others enumerated above; collecting the feathers may have been a tedious job, not nearly so amusing or satisfactory as shell-collecting, for instance. A certain amount of knowledge of ornithology would be needed for some of its branches, and the storing of the feathers themselves may have presented some problems. We know that many charming cabinets were made specially to house shells and quartzes; but I have never seen – or even heard of any piece specially designed to hold feathers.

The Misses Parminter (mentioned later in this chapter), who did a tremendous amount of feather-work, seemed to have kept the smaller feathers in folded pieces of note-paper, stored in cardboard boxes, for I was shown some delicate feathers preserved in this way when I visited 'à la Ronde'.

I imagine – along with many other things which we value

nowadays – a great deal was swept out of their houses by Edwardian housewives in their great revolt against 'Victorian rubbish'. Unfortunately for succeeding generations, much was ruthlessly destroyed under this heading, when in fact it was neither Victorian nor rubbish, and we have lost forever many things which should have been preserved. In fact – although it is difficult to believe in this informed age – the process is still going on. I have been horrified over and over again by hearing of valuable articles thrown in the dust-bin or burnt on the garden bonfire with the sorry excuse – "We didn't know it was worth anything." In this way, to my certain knowledge, have gone 18th-century dolls and doll's-houses, a Chippendale chest-of-drawers, yew-tree Windsor chairs, early oak settles, glass lustres and needlework, to mention only a few such things that spring to mind. Almost every talk I give on the subject of antiques brings forth a fresh crop. I suppose we should count ourselves lucky that, in spite of all this, so much has been carefully preserved. One such thing I saw recently which had had a lucky escape was an early Victorian album. In it – among pressed flowers, skeleton leaves and seaweed, I came across several pages devoted to a simple form of feather-work which was most attractive. The middle of each page contained a different brightly coloured bird cut out from a cheap print (or Christmas card). Round the bird, like a frame, was a slender wreath of delicate feathers in various colours. None of them were more than about 4 inches long, and the pictures thus made were striking and effective; they would have looked charming framed as a set.

Bird pictures

The most favoured way of using feathers was turning them into pictures of the birds themselves. There are two or three different variations of these, the simplest being those where, so to speak, feathers are used instead of paint. The birds are drawn on a plain paper background, and then filled in with the appropriate coloured feathers, starting from the tail, and building towards the neck, so that the quill end is never

Plate 15

Bird Picture in Feather-work.

seen. The final neck feathers are covered by very much smaller feathers which, starting at the beak, come down to join the neck feathers (Plate 15). Such birds as canaries, thrushes, blue tits, yellow hammers, etc. were the favourites, with only one, or at the most two birds portrayed in each picture. Large birds were also attempted. I have seen birds such as cocks and hens, partridges and pheasants, and other game-birds portrayed about one-half their natural size. The right feathering is rigidly adhered to, and very natural backgrounds are just sketched in. Various kinds of frames are used. As the feathers are not padded in any way there is no need for a box-frame.

Later another type of large bird model was made. In this case the bodies were padded before the feathers were applied, to give a rounded effect, and glass beads were often used for the eyes. The background was of blue or green-washed paper, occasionally with some real grasses to make it more naturalistic, and the whole was inserted in a box-frame. Some of these are attractive and life-like pieces of work, but a greater number are unnatural looking and appear very amateurish.

Feathers used as mural decorations

Although I have mentioned the house, 'à la Ronde', in the previous chapters, I refrained from giving a full description of it. It is in this house that one can see a unique display of feather work executed in the late 18th and early 19th centuries. The house was built in 1791 by two ladies – the Misses Parminter, who, having visited Italy, and seen the round church of San Vitale at Ravenna, decided to build a round house on the same principle. This house is intensely interesting architecturally, and its interior decoration even more so. One notable instance of this is the cornice round the drawing-room ceiling, of a classic design worked in short coloured feathers. The cornice is over a foot wide, and the effect unusual and highly original. The same form of decoration, on a much smaller scale, runs round the fire-place – giving those interested a chance to see how the feathers are worked. Naturally they are a good deal more the worse for wear in such a place, though attempts have been made from time to time to repair the decoration.

In the drawing-room also are two very well-executed pictures of yellow-feathered birds on white paper backgrounds. In another downstairs room are some small stuffed birds in a glass case. In fact I believe these birds had no real existence at all, but were actually composed of feathers built up on frame-work figures. They are perched naturalistically on little twigs, and the feathers are of very gay colours.

Having climbed up some steep and narrow stairs, built in the thickness of the wall, one comes to a breathtaking gallery, which runs all round the inner wall at the top of the house. (If you have a dread of heights, don't look down into the hall below!) There are several windows set in embrasures at intervals round this gallery from which the most beautiful views of the Exe estuary and surrounding countryside can be seen.

Plate 16
Feather and Shell-work Murals at 'à la Ronde', Exmouth. Late 18th cent.

These embrasures are covered with different designs in local shells; but the shell panels on the walls between alternate with feather panels, mostly of full-sized large birds in profile on the wall (Plate 16). Time here has wrought many ravages, but in a way this is a help to the student, for one can now tell exactly the way in which the birds were made, and in what order the feathers were fixed. In one case – a partridge I believe – the soft part of the bird's feathers have been stuck to the outline drawn previously on the wall, and the feathers built up – neckwards – on this foundation.

When one contemplates all the various mediums – shell, paper, sand, seaweed and feather – these ladies worked in, one cannot see how they had time to accomplish it all, as it was not begun until they were over forty; and this was by no means all they did – for needlework pictures, silhouettes, etc., are also in evidence. Happily some very good photographs of the interior of 'à la Ronde' have been taken – which can go on record; because the feather-work cannot last forever, indeed it is astonishing that it has lasted so long, unglazed and exposed as it is to dust, moth and sea-air.

It was a fashionable thing in the Georgian days to decorate one's rooms with feathers – as part of the integral scheme. The poet Cowper, who must often have attended the literary salon in Portman Square of Mrs. Elizabeth Montague (the first of the 'blue-stockings'), wrote the following lines on the subject:

"*On Mrs. Montague's Feather Hangings*"
The birds put off their every hue
To dress a room for Montague
The Peacock sends his heavenly dyes,
His rainbows and his starry eyes;
The Pheasant plumes, which round infold
His mantling neck with downy gold;
The cock his arched tail's azure show;
And, river-blanched, the Swan his snow,
All tribes beside of Indian name
That glossy shine, or vivid flame,
Where rises and where sets the day,
Whate'er they boast of rich and gay,
Contribute to the gorgeous plan
Proud to advance it all they can.
This plumage neither dashing shower,
Nor blasts, that shake the dripping bower
Shall drench again or discompose,
But, screened from every storm that blows,
It boasts a splendour ever new,
Safe with protecting Montague."

These lines remind us that at this period no house of any size was complete without its aviary. Here peacocks, birds of paradise, canaries, parrots and other exotic birds were housed, or allowed to roam at will on the lawns and terraces. With the coming of landscape gardening, a certain amount of colour, normally obtained from flower-beds, had been lost; and to make up for this deficiency – as well as to supply a romantic note – exotic birds had been imported. Although the 'genteel female' would have scorned to keep anything as common as poultry, an aviary of exotic birds was quite another matter, and something which – no doubt with plenty of aid from the staff – she felt no loss of dignity in

Plate 17
Nosegay in Feather-work.

tending. The birds moulted in due season, and a supply of coloured feathers was thus always available.

Another venue was the plucked feathers from birds dressed ready for cooking. Poultry and game-birds were eaten in large quantities at this time, and there can have been no scarcity.

Feather-nosegays

This form of feather-work is probably the most skilful form, and perhaps the most beautiful. I do not think there can be a better example than the one in Plate 17. It is a companion to the shell-nosegay in Plate 2, and framed in exactly the same way. When one speaks of feather work one is accustomed to think of the whole of the feather being used; but in this case each flower petal is composed of cut feathers mounted (in the case of roses and dahlias) on rounded bases, such as dried thistle or teazel heads. In fact the leaves and the stalks in this nosegay look as if they might belong to the thistle or teazel family and are suitably tinted. The shell-nosegay is astonishing in its verisimilitude to the real thing, but this feather-nosegay is almost unbelievable. Tiny pieces of feathers in their natural colours are cut to the shape of each particular petal needed, and various fronds which are mixed in with the very colourful flowers could be the spines of feathers curled (as one curls ostrich feathers) by running a knife blade down the spine.

The finished nosegay is tied with a true lover's-knot made of tiny pieces of white feather glued to a leather foundation (to make it appear like stiff white ribbon). This 'ribbon' has been embroidered in feather moss-rose buds.

Such a piece must always have been kept under glass, or it would never have survived so fresh and vivid to this day.

Feather tippets

Just as the 20th-century Edwardian ladies loved to wear neck scarves made of small feathers – known as 'feather boas' – so apparently did 18th-century ladies of fashion like to wear tippets made of feathers. We read that in 1727 Mrs. Delany sent her sister Anne a tippet "of her own making and invention." Mr. Brimley Johnson, who mentions this in his book, says in a footnote that he thinks the tippet must have been made of feathers, and adds, "A most beautiful tippet of this description has been preserved, and is still in existence. It is long, narrow and flat, lined with white satin, made to fit the neck, and fall with long ends over the chest. The principal feathers are those of the macaw, dark blue gentianello colour, relieved with scarlet, and interspersed with small feathers of the canary bird."

During this period people were very "feather-conscious". Even fine dessert services were decorated with designs of feathers, and small strong feathers were used as the spokes of fans. (A hundred years later ostrich feathers were being used for this same purpose, and very elegant they were too.)

Birds of paradise, peacocks, and parrots were favourite birds for the artist to portray – not only on canvas, but on papier-mâché trays, fire-screens and small pieces of furniture. Several notable artists – celebrated for their bird studies, were employed by well-known firms in Birmingham and Wolverhampton to paint trays from about 1820 onwards, and the beautiful work they turned out decorates our walls to this day.

4 HAIR-WORK

Hair embroidery in French Canada and Europe

Although hair for the purposes of decoration does not seem to have been used in Europe much before the 18th century, it had been used long before this in North America by the Indians to decorate their moccasins, belts and pouches. Highly stylised and original patterns were worked out, in which moose and elk hairs were 'couched' on to the garment with white cotton thread. White moose hair was used with effect, but other hairs were dyed, and the embroidery was enriched with small portions of porcupine quills.

Towards the end of the 17th century some intrepid Ursuline nuns from France came to Quebec to educate the native Indian girls. Three of these dedicated women were expert embroideresses, and they started to teach their pupils the art of embroidery; the necessary silks and gilt thread being ordered from France. After a time it became necessary to economise and they tried to find a local substitute for the silk.

It was perhaps natural that having seen, and doubtless taken great interest in, the native embroidery, they should start to experiment with moose hair. But they completely set aside the Indian technique of merely 'couching' on several strands of hair as a border or outline stitch, and kept to their European traditions by using single strands of the hair to embroider their designs in the same way as they would have used silk. This was an enormously tedious and difficult job, as the hairs were short in length compared with silk, and very slippery. To combat the slipperiness they backed their material with thin strips of bark – or thick-corded silk – which closed round the hair, holding it more firmly. The shortness they contended with by pushing the needle nearly through the material before threading it; this meant that it had to be re-threaded after almost every stitch. The hair was prepared for use by dyeing with vegetable dyes, and then bundled together in hanks. It was wetted immediately before use to make it more tensile.

This effort at economy produced an entirely new method of embroidery, quite unlike any other. 'Satin' stitch was used extensively; and as berries played a large part in the various designs, 'French Knots' were used to give the knobbly texture. This called for even more patience, as moose hair could not be thought an ideal thread for making such a stitch – which is complicated even with embroidery silk.

The nuns' embroidery was originally meant for the adornment of vestments, altar frontals, banners, etc., but later small secular things, such as purses, belts and card-cases, were made commercially – and the embroidery was done directly on the bark.

Other religious communities started convent schools in Quebec, Trois-Rivières and Montreal, where daughters of French colonists were taught this embroidery. It was also done by French-Canadian ladies.

The French fur-trappers became good customers, as their picturesque style of dress required a great deal of embroidery. And, much earlier than one would have imagined, this convent hair-embroidery work was brought over to Europe, where it became known as 'Indian Curios'. It reached its best period about 1830.

I was very anxious to obtain some photographs of this work if possible, as it is difficult to describe, so I got in touch with the French-Canadian Museum at Quebec to see if they could help me. While I was awaiting their answer, however, I was thrilled to come across one of these 'Indian Curios'. I should say it was intended to be a spectacle case, and is an interesting example of the traditional stitch and design originated by the Ursuline nuns. The design has been worked

te 18
ectacle-case in Moose-hair embroidered bark. Canadian. Circa 1830.

Plate 19
Pin-cushion in Moose-hair embroidered on bark. Canadian. Circa 1830.

directly on to the bark, and I should judge the date to be about 1830 (Plates 18 and 19).

About a fortnight later I found the pretty little pin-cushion in (Plates 18 and 19), tucked away in a glass cabinet in a country antique shop. An interesting feature of this 'export' work is that though the design of embroidery in the main is European, the old Indian method of 'couching' has been used to join the two sides together.

Did this influx of moose-hair embroidery suggest to the European ladies the use of human hair in embroidery and horse-hair as an alternative to crochet cotton? Or was it just a curious coincidence that about this time the use of both these materials came into fashion?

Whatever the reason, 18th-century English school-girls were enhancing a certain type of very fine embroidery – done to emulate etching – by the introduction of human hair. I

Plate 20
Picture of 'GIRL with DOVE'. Worked in human hair on satin.

have such a picture at the moment. It is worked in tiny stitches with black silk on a white satin ground, and depicts a girl standing before an open cage of doves. The light shading on her hair and dress is done with pale gold hair, which shimmers if the picture is moved about. Round her left wrist a piece of twine is loosely coiled. This is in fact a length of dark hair (Plate 20).

I have seen a very fine sampler worked in coloured silks, with the usual verse at the end necessary to samplers of that period, followed by an oval containing the child's name, age and school. All the lettering is worked in a minute cross-stitch with what appears to be extremely fine black thread, but a label on the back states that it was worked in hair. I think it is of interest to give the text here:

> Had I the world at my command,
> The treasures of the sea and land,
> And should I all the world bestow
> It would not pay the debt I owe.
>
> Eliza Yates aged 9
> years, done at
> Sileby School 1809

Poor little soul! At nine years old to feel burdened with such a debt – and for what? The benefits of a school that instilled such ideas into children's minds? No wonder youth has rebelled.

Human hair was a fashionable introduction into jewellery at this time. Not only for insertion in mourning rings and lockets, but for hair bracelets. These were of hair made into a coil on a round loom like the ones children make with cotton-reels and tacks. I had one of brown hair which formed the middle part of the bracelet. One end was fixed into a snake's head, modelled in gold studded with turquoises, while the other end terminated in the snake's tail which was being held in the snake's mouth. (This was an old emblem of eternity, and a favourite design for such jewellery in the Regency period.) The hair coil was 'springy', which enabled it to stretch a little when pulled over the hand.

Human hair was also used in place of silk in embroidery pictures. The most interesting one I have seen was in the form of a flower picture.* The stalks and leaves were worked in different shades of hair which were 'couched' on to a white satin background. The flowers were formed of different-sized pearls, the whole bunch being tied together with a piece of pale blue ribbon tied in a true lover's-knot.

I thought at the time that this had been done at a girl's school as a souvenir – each girl donating so much of her hair. One wonders where all this human hair came from, but it must not be forgotten that in the early 19th century it was the

* *This form of hair embroidery must have been used in France, for there is a similar sort of picture in the Peterborough Museum made by a French prisoner-of-war at Norman Cross prison.*

fashion for girls and young women to have their hair cropped, so that there must have been a fair amount of this material available. Perhaps doting mothers collected the shorn tresses, and by using it in this way had a perpetual reminder of their daughters' 'crowning glory'.

There was once a romantic fashion of embroidering the initials of one's loved one on cambric or lawn handkerchiefs with one's own hair – a rather charming idea which I hope was properly appreciated.

Horse-hair work

A common commodity in the 18th and 19th centuries for stuffing seats and backs of furniture, as well as for making certain types of wigs, black horse-hair was also woven into a stout shiny material for the outer covers on furniture. It must have been extremely hard wearing, for original covers are still found on Regency and early Victorian chairs to this day. It had the disadvantages of being very slippery and rather prickly. In the 1930s a modern variant was made: a large amount of wool and cotton was interwoven with the hair which made it soft, supple and more usable, with the advantage of being obtainable in various colours.

As horse-hair was always available, it is not surprising to find that it was used for making cheap watch-chains, muff-chains, bracelets and rings. The rings had names worked into them and sold at sixpence each – probably at fairs and on stalls at markets. Watch- and muff-chains were made of plaited horse-hair made into linked circles. Such things were very light in weight, and therefore easily lost, so that very little of the work has survived.

White horse-hair was used as a kind of crocheting thread for unusual work of a very beautiful kind. The bracelet depicted in Plate 21 is a real work of art. The hair has yellowed slightly with age, imparting a pale creamy tinge which is very attractive – rather like carved ivory but much lighter in weight and more comfortable to wear. The hair is worked into a kind of lace stitch with the flowers standing up quite boldly from the ground-work. The stamens of each

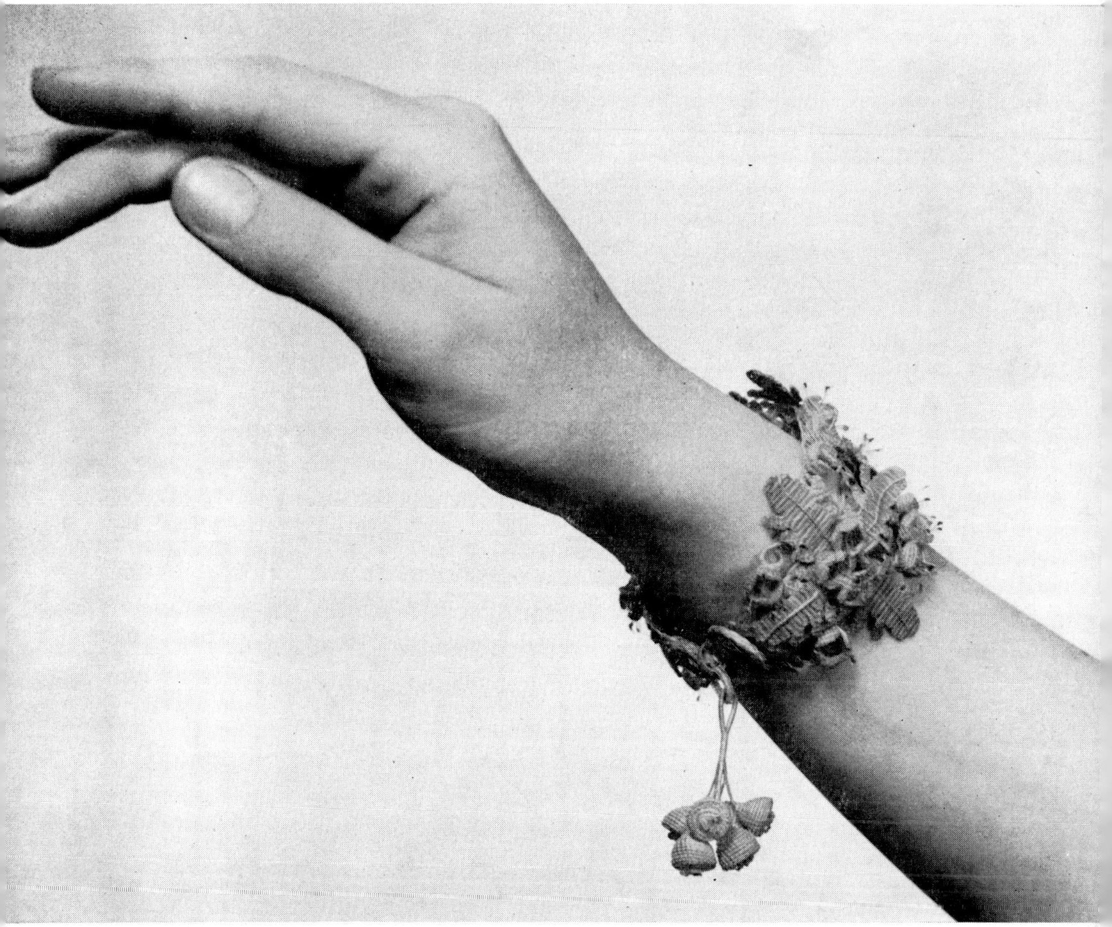

Plate 21
White Horse-hair Bracelet, Regency period.

flower are tinged with chinese red. This bracelet is easily secured by buttons and loops of the same material. It is one of a pair of the Regency period, but I have no idea of the country of origin, though Spain has been suggested.

5 FELT-WORK PICTURES

Towards the end of the 18th century there seems to have been a fondness for using a dark material as the background for needlework pictures of fruit and flowers. I imagine this was probably due to the influence of the beautiful Pontypool enamelled tin goods that at this time were so fashionable. Most of these things – chestnut vases, tea and coffee urns, etc. – were decorated in gilt on chocolate brown or black backgrounds. Henry Clay's improved papier-mâché trays of a rich black lacquer were decorated in colour, and these were highly popular – not only for use, but for ornament, and the idea may have sprung from them.

At a country house sale in Devon a few years ago three flower pictures were sold, all worked in bright colours on dull black satin backgrounds. Two were a pair depicting fruit and flowers in baskets, and the third had for its subject a vase of variegated flowers. They were all framed in Georgian frames of gilded wood, which seems to have been the accepted way of framing this type of picture.

A rather more curious and unusual background was of brown felt. This was almost always used in conjunction with appliqué-work in coloured felts – or occasionally velvet. Although appliqué-work had been done for centuries in one form or another, this type was an innovation. A favourite design was a basket, worked in a straw-coloured silk or chenille, from which flowed an abundance of fruit or flowers in different coloured felts appliquéd on with embroidery silk. The fruits were padded slightly to give the right shape, and the shadings and high-lights indicated with embroidered stitching. Fruit done in this way is particularly realistic.

In some cases velvet appliqué replaced that of felt. We had a delightful picture of a basket of strawberries, in which the fruit itself was made of padded velvet, with the seeds embroidered on in silk, and the leaves were of green felt. The basket was worked in a straw-coloured chenille, and was about 2 inches deep so that it was fairly bursting with most natural-looking fruit. The very deep box-frame was of the usual gold, and the background of brown felt. It dated from the period 1790–1800.

Baskets (or vases) of flowers were fashionable also, but the method of making them was slightly different. The flowers and leaves were all fashioned out of felt – each petal separately done – and stood away from the receptacle, which held them in a naturalistic manner.

There are exceptions to the usual appliqué-work of felt on felt. Very occasionally the felt background was used for fine silk embroidery. The most beautiful example of this was one which passed through our hands – a portrait of the head and shoulders of a young girl with long fair hair, wearing a dress of the early 19th century. This was worked with fine pale-coloured silks on a very dark-brown felt background, and framed in an oval gilt frame. The unusual combination of pastel coloured, almost hair-fine silks on brown felt give an almost ethereal quality to the child's face that is utterly charming.

We once bought a pair of pictures that had been on Georgian pole-screens (backed in the usual way with pleated red silk), which consisted of two panels of Stuart needlework, mounted on dark-brown felt with narrow gilt braid. The panels, which were extremely fine, had probably been part of a casket. Using such a background, which to us nowadays would seem quite inappropriate, indicates that at that time brown felt must have been the fashionable material for this purpose.

The one great disadvantage of felt as a needlework background is that damage is often found to have been done to it by woodworm. I thought at first that the holes I kept finding in such pieces were due to moth – though I could not understand how moth could penetrate through a glass front and wood backing. However, on taking one picture to pieces to mend the fabric, I discovered worm-holes in the wood backing. The worms had penetrated through the wood, and the holes in the felt beneath exactly corresponded with them. Luckily the worms had only attacked the edge of the backing, so the damage was not as noticeable as it might have been. I find it safer now to remove all wood backing from needlework pictures, and substitute a thick hard cardboard. This trouble with worm applies not only to needlework pictures– but almost to everything that is backed by thin or three-ply wood: mirrors, watercolours, prints, etc. Worms love this thin wood, and through it they make inroads into the frames themselves, especially into those made of fruitwood or walnut. They work secretly there for months, undisturbed and unnoticed. One can see the action of woodworm in furniture – but one somehow neglects to examine the backs of picture and mirror-frames for it. It is a real danger, however, and one which should be guarded against. There are people who exclaim with horror at an ancient hole in a piece of early oak furniture from which theworm escaped hundreds of years ago – but are blissfully ignorant about the live worm that is rampant in the three-ply backing of the modern mirrors on their walls.

Moths of course will attack material when only a paper backing has been used which has perished or been torn. If the holes occur, as they often seem to do, near the edge of the picture, it is possible to conceal them by applying a narrow antique braid all round the edge. If, as sometimes happens, they appear in some more conspicuous place, then the more difficult job of trying to match up the colour and substance of the material with a piece of backing has to be tackled. If they occur anywhere near actual felt appliqué-work, then perhaps a little judicious appliqué patch in the form of a fruit or flower can be done. This must fall naturally and appropriately into place however. Disguising blemishes can sometimes be a mistake – like that made by a misguided Edwardian lady who painted gaily coloured butterflies in oils over every dark spot on the original Vauxhall glass of a large and important Chippendale mirror that graced her drawing-room.

6 FLUTED-EMBROIDERY WORK

Orné wool-work

I have been careful to include in this book the more unusual type of handiwork our ancestresses engaged in. Many books have been written on embroidery that include wool-work such as tapestries, samplers, cut-wool work, etc., and it would be unnecessary for me to include descriptions of them here. I will content myself with describing one or two variants that do not usually find their way into such books for one reason or another.

I suppose that most women engaged presently in making tapestry covers for chairs or stools do not realise that it is only comparatively recently that canvases for working on have been marked out and coloured in, all ready for the embroideress to begin her work without the tedium of having to do such a chore for herself.

In the early days of wool-work, the ladies had to mark out their own patterns on the canvas. If they were not clever enough to design the pattern for themselves, coloured ones could be obtained. But these had to be copied from an illustration, and drawn laboriously, square by square, on to a piece of plain canvas, with the colours either indicated or painted in. My mother had two or three such designs which she had inherited from a great-aunt, and she amused herself by copying them on to the canvases she wished to work, which was far from simple. Unfortunately, all these old designs are now lost so I am unable to give any illustrations of them. They were all for chair seats and stools, but there were

Plate 22
One of a Pair of Wool-work Slippers. Victorian.

others for such unusual things (to us) as the gentlemen's slippers, in Plate 22, braces and watch pockets to hang on the curtain at the back of the bed.

Years ago I used to buy up pieces of Regency and Victorian wool-work to make up into cushions. In those days they were cheap and plentiful, but everybody since then has had the same idea, so that now it is hardly possible to buy them at all, at any price. Most of this wool-work was straightforward cross-stitch on canvas, but there was a variant of it I never understood. It seemed to me almost like machine-made tapestry, and yet I felt sure it was hand-made. Also it was practically the same on both sides, and I did not understand how this effect could possibly have been obtained so neatly. It was not until quite recently, when I found a volume of the *Ladies' Companion* for 1857, that I discovered how it was done – and that it was called *Fluted Embroidery*.

The vital difference between this wool-work and any other kind was that the design was painted on the wool itself, and worked on a plain canvas. The embroideress, provided that she followed the instructions with extreme care, would find that the design appeared on both sides of the canvas as she

Plate 23
Wool-work picture of flowers in 'Fluted Embroidery'. Victorian. From the 'Ladies' Companion' for 1857.

worked – I imagine this must have been a most fascinating pastime. The wool was known as *Orné* wool, and a picture of the finished embroidery is given in Plate 23.

The following extract is taken from an article called 'The Work-table' in the aforementioned magazine.

GROUP OF FLOWERS IN FLUTED EMBROIDERY

"We give a drawing of a beautiful new fabric, termed 'fluted embroidery'. This unique style of needlework is performed by a peculiar method of sewing over cord, on railway canvas, producing the same elegant design on both sides of the fabric, which is inimitable by any other mode of working.

"The Orné wool has the design printed on it, and is wound in a ball, consisting of many threads of wool, of equal length, each length forming a row. The canvas has been especially manufactured for the purpose, and is much finer than any hitherto produced. It is dyed sage-green, so that the tint does not injure the effect of the shading of the wool. Each piece is divided into four spaces by red threads, which greatly assists the worker, as each space works up a quarter of the length of wool. The cord is fixed on each side of the canvas alternately inverting the work for each fresh row, always commencing in the centre of the canvas, with the middle of the wool, sewing the first half with the finished part held to you (for every specimen sold is already commenced) always putting in the needle to the right, and drawing it through to the left, measuring as directed in the instructions which accompany each piece, for every quarter length of wool, and insuring a correct development of the pattern as the work proceeds. It is one of the prettiest novelties we have seen for some time, and commends itself equally for its beauty and durability."

The Orné wool was not only used as a medium for embroidery but, as one can readily imagine, as a knitting wool, and I feel that I must include the knitting pattern for an 'Anti-macassar or couvre-pieds' in this chapter. (The word

Plate 24
Knitted Anti-macassar in Orné Wool-work. Victorian. From the 'Ladies' Companion' for 1857.

'couvre-pieds' is new to me, but its sense is quite obvious – I wonder why it did not last as long as its fellow word 'antimacassar'!)

The design (pictured in Plate 24) is worked as follows:

> "With a skein of claret Berlin wool, cast on 210 stitches. Then fasten on the Orné-wool and knit one row in moss-stitch. This stitch has a peculiarly soft and mossy appearance, and no material is so well calculated to develop its beauty as the Orné knitting-wool. In this new wool the design works out with all the accuracy and beauty of painting; and it is a singular fact, applying equally to this and the fluted embroidery, that the colours, instead of fading from wear, become considerably brighter.
>
> "When four plain rows in the moss-stitch are done, the colours will begin to form a pattern.
>
> 5th row. 17 stitches green, 7 brown, 33 green, 3 brown, 45 green; then count backwards.
>
> 6th row. 16 green, 14 brown, 20 green, 2 brown, 4 green, 5 brown, 2 green, 3 brown, 36 green; then count backwards.
>
> 7th row. 14 green, 20 brown, 9 green, 4 brown, 2 green, 4 brown, 3 green, 5 brown, 1 green, 6 brown, 31 green, 3 brown, 3 green; then count backwards.
>
> "Regular knitting will now perfectly ensure a proper development of the pattern. If the knot which should come in the wool at the end of every row, does not occur in its place, the latter stitches must be either tightened or slackened with the finger without undoing the work.
>
> "A round of treble crochet, in shaded amber wool should afterwards be worked all round the anti-macassar; and an Orné fringe be knotted in at regular intervals.
>
> MATERIALS: Orné knitting ball 15. Wood or bone needles No. 12."

This Orné wool must have been expensive to obtain, or else following the patterns was too difficult for most people, because examples worked in it very rarely turn up, and I have

never been fortunate enough to find an unused ball of wool.

While we are on the subject of wool-work, I would like to write a little about the influence this Victorian craze had on furniture and furnishings. There were, for instance, special tables made especially for the wool-work enthusiasts. These were small round tables with wooden pillared galleries 3 or 4 inches high which went round the table-top. Sometimes there was a lower tier, also galleried; these were for holding the balls securely. Also the colours could be readily seen and picked out when wanted. For some curious reason these tables are often referred to as 'wine-tables' – just as the narrow wooden galleried trays with handles at each end made to hold balls of wool, are known as either wine or book trays. Then there were shallow oval open baskets made of

Plate 25
Silhouette of the Parminter Family by Torond. 18th cent.

cane, or a late form of papier-mâché, known as 'bread baskets'. They may be so used now, but the Victorians would have scorned to use such commonplace things on their tables or sideboards.

Perhaps the most ridiculous name is that given to the beautiful painted little round trays of papier-mâché which may have been for visiting cards. If so, why do they have carrying handles of ormolu? One does not want to carry visiting cards about with one from room to room. But even this is better than calling them 'cake-trays'. Cakes were served on porcelain cake-plates, small ones in silver baskets. Papier-mâché would be a most unsuitable material for holding confectionary; on the other hand, it would make a light and charming container for wool.

7 WAX MODELLING

When I first started to write this book I knew my readers would expect me to include a chapter on wax-flower modelling. This I thought would not be a difficult task. There would be no dearth of information on the subject, and surely it would be easy to find a model one could photograph and describe. I had a vague recollection of having seen several such wax-flower models under glass domes from time to time, but as soon as I began to look for a good model I realised it was not going to be as simple as I had thought. I tracked glass domes down whenever I saw them lurking at the back of shops that might be supposed to stock such things – and I found plenty. They housed dolls, paper flower arrangements, stuffed birds, tree sprays adorned with butterflies, ornamental grasses, models of Swiss chalets, copies of the Taj Mahal, prisoner-of-war bone models, spun-glass objects and many other things – but not wax flowers. As these seemed the most appropriate 'works-of-art' to be under glass, and hundreds must have been made, I could not understand what had happened to them all. Then I learnt that the best and earliest of these flower models were arranged in fine alabaster vases – and this immediately gave me a clue. Some years ago a vogue was started for doing real flower arrangements in alabaster containers – and also one for making lamps out of tall alabaster vases big enough for the purpose (very often these had an internal bulb which when lit gave a charming translucent effect). The wax flowers had therefore been thrown away. The domed glass stands were used for other purposes, and the alabaster vases, still immaculate from having been preserved from dust and damage for so long, were now put on a ready market. They turn up every so often, but the course of time has considerably added to their value.

As I was anxious to include a picture of wax flowers, I decided to give one of a flower picture in wax. This attractive work was done by Emmanuel M. Dieman,* 1768–90, and I think it conveys exactly the artistry that can be achieved in this medium (Frontispiece).

I had thought also that it would be fairly simple to come across recipes for making the wax flowers; but my search went on for months. Then I finally came across an amusing little early Victorian manual published in 1844 and called simply *Modelling Wax Flowers*, by John and Horatio Mintorn. These youthful gentlemen describe themselves modestly in the preface as being very young to undertake to teach the art, but say also that they are relying on the fact that they had learnt it from their parents, who have been in the top rank of wax modellers.

This book was exactly what I had been hoping to find, as the methods described in it would be professional ones, probably widely used in the 18th century, and therefore worthy of note.

The Mintorn brothers lived at 36 Soho Square, and had a 'counter' in the Pantheon in Oxford Street. These counters were the forerunners of stalls in the 19th-century bazaars, and not unlike the small stands in antique markets of the present day.

From these two addresses they were able to supply all the necessary materials their pupils would require. And their little manual, as well as being educational, was a clever advertisement for their wares. It is amusing to see that even then a hint that nobility was interested in their products was thought to be an excellent inducement for the public to buy them.

The nobility in this case appears in the somewhat fulsome dedication, which reads:

* *A German artist working in England.*

"TO HER GRACE, the
Duchess of Northumberland.
To Whose
Encouraging Patronage
We are deeply indebted
THIS SMALL VOLUME
is, with
Her Grace's Condescending Permission
most respectfully dedicated
by Her Grace's
Ever grateful
And very humble servants
JOHN and HORATIO MINTORN"

After a rather long preface, the authors proceed to describe their method of modelling wax flowers as follows:

MODELLING WAX FLOWERS

List of Essential Materials for making Wax Flowers.

1. Patterns of the various petals etc. To be procured at Mr. Mintorn's counter in the Pantheon, Oxford St.
2. A pair of light and thin scissors (such as are used by surgeons).
3. A cup to hold water.
4. A flat earthenware Palette.
5. A steel Curling Pin, 5 inches in length, with a globular head of glass.
6. Eight bottles of colour in powder form, 3 shades of yellow, one white, a crimson or Rose tint, and 3 shades of Blue. One Bottle of White and 1 of Green down.
7. A dozen brushes all of one size. One brush is necessary for each particular tint.
8. Three or four different sized small sable brushes.
9. A dozen Sheets of Wax. White, Lemon, Yellow, Pink, light and dark Green.

10. Wires of three different sizes.
11. A cake of Crimson Lake.
12. A cake of Sepia.

METHOD OF MODELLING

"Before you commence cutting out, take care to render your Scissors loose in the rivet. Dip them constantly in the cup of water at your side, to prevent their adhesion to the wax; should they, in spite of this, become clogged, place them in your mouth for a few seconds, and the heat will clear the edge.

"The wax has a dull and a glossy side. The paper patterns must be laid upon the dull side, so that in cutting out, you secure a sharp and clear edge; be cautious that you place the pattern in such a position as to cut with the grain of the wax.

"Spread half a sheet of tissue paper over the table upon which you intend to work, so as to prevent the slightest dust, smut or grease from injuring the purity of your wax. Take up with the point of your curling pin the portions as you use them, and thereby prevent any unnecessary handling. Great attention should be bestowed on the mixing of the colours. . . . (Here follow hints on how to obtain various shades.) Take, with a small palette knife or spatula, out of the bottle a minute portion of the required colour, and dip the end of the brush stick into water, letting the globule fall upon the palette near the powder, and mix well together until the required tint be of the consistency of cream, and perfectly smooth.

"We must caution our readers against ever dipping the body of the brush or bristles, into water. The various brushes used, are held perfectly upright, with the colour applied somewhat rapidly over the wax, taking care to go with the grain. Be ever careful to avoid covering with your tint that portion of the petal which is to be joined to the foundation of the flower, as any moisture or colour prevents a proper and secure adhesion."

Directions are then given for modelling each of the following flowers:

Yellow Rose	Moss Rose
Orange and White Azalias	Fuchsia
Yellow and White Jasmine	Laburnam
White Camelia	Dahlia
Purple Rose	Carnation
Passion Flower	Pink Geranium
Violet	Crocus

Curiously enough the most difficult flowers to do are given first, so that the pupil should learn all the most difficult steps. I have selected the *White Camelia* as a specimen because the instructions appear fairly simple.

Formation of a White Camelia

"The leaves, having been cut out of thick wax are coloured. The small petals alone require colour. The camelia must be constructed on the largest size wire; the end intended to support the flower must be bent five times backwards and forwards, each bend a quarter of an inch. Half a sheet of White Wax is then rolled round the twisted and compressed wire till it attains the size of a plum-stone. (This is to prevent the possibility of the stem slipping from the flower.) Dip the curling-pin in water. Place the petal flat on the 1st finger of the left hand. The curling-pin is to be held in the right so as to rest upon the centre of the upper part of the thumb. To give the actual concavity to each petal, roll the head of the pin close to the edge of the portion of the wax in use. Having done this, place the point of the pin in the centre, and consult your taste and judgement till you perceive that you have obtained the required natural form. The first 3 petals are attached close to the plum-stone shaped wax. The 4 following rows, curled similar to the others, are so arranged that each is a little higher than the other so as to avoid one leaf growing absolutely at the back of the other.

"On arriving at the 6th size, the pin's point is placed upon the *dull* side of the wax, so as to turn the petals backwards. These and their successors are to be placed a little below the work already completed.

"Using the appropriate pattern, our next step is the making of the calyx.

"It should be made of primrose coloured wax, and then coloured on the dull side with a delicate green, the edges carefully touched with a light purplish brown. The sepals, or leaves of the calyx are first curled upon the glossy side, and then on the dull one, that the edges may turn back. The 3 largest are applied close to the back of the flower, and the small ones so placed as to form a double trefoil."

The Stalk

"Take a strip of green wax and roll and press it tightly round the wire, and a tint of purple brown colour should be applied. Two or three leaves are then placed upon the stalk and the flower is complete.

"*Alabaster vases* are the most suitable backgrounds for the varied hues of the flowers, and glass shades are absolutely essential for ladies who desire to preserve the work of their fair hands. All these can be obtained on most reasonable terms from our counter, also a supply of wax and cambric leaves."

The alabaster vases were imported specially from abroad by the Mintorns, in various shapes and designs, and it was urged on their fair customers to buy all the wax, etc. needed from their counter at the Pantheon to ensure that they got the very best obtainable. Workers in wax were warned not to use the 'cake' paints on the petals, as the paint was too thick, and spoilt the transparency of the wax.

I wonder if there are any curling-sticks left? I should dearly like to try to model the wax flowers from the recipes given. I feel sure, however, that modern materials would not produce the same effect at all. Powder paints can still be found, and I have used them for ordinary watercolours, having been presented with a whole painting outfit dating from about 1830 that had both powder and 'cake' paints, brushes and pencils of that period. But I fear that the Mintorns' 'Wax Sheets' must have disappeared many many years ago.

Shortly after reading the Mintorns' book, I discovered, through the kind interest of a friend, that a book on the same subject had been written twelve years later in 1856 by a Mrs. Emma Peachey – described as 'artiste to Her Majesty'. This book is called *The Royal Guide to Wax Flower Modelling*, and though she describes herself as being self-taught, her method hardly differs at all from that of the Mintorns. She was undoubtedly herself a superb wax-modeller, and prepared two wonderful exhibits for the Great Exhibition at the Crystal Palace in Hyde Park. These, however, were never shown there, as the position allotted to her was in the Gallery – much too near the heat from the glass roof for the safety of the wax fruit and flower arrangements. However, she held a private exhibition of them at her house – 35 Rathbone Place and it was "visited by 50,000 people."

Mrs. Peachey had 'counters' in the Soho bazaar where her own materials could be purchased for home modelling, on which subject she had the following to say:

> "One great consideration of the advantage of wax-modelling over other fancy work is that the sight is not likely to be injured . . . nor need the body be *bent*, – a matter of much importance with growing girls, many having suffered affections of the chest, and others disfigured for life, through continually stooping to frame-work."

She also says:

> "It is perfectly clear according to my method, that the most elegant drawing-room might be used, without suffering in its appearance during its operations. I would merely recommend that the table should be covered with paper, so that all small pieces might be kept together, and easily removed."

She has one very interesting fact to relate – that the art of wax-modelling was introduced into this country from Italy by the mother of Mary of Modena, second wife of James II, in 1686. This lady had some very fine wax-work models of fruit and flowers, said to have been made by nuns, put up in her daughter's chapel and rooms.

Finally, I cannot better close this chapter than by quoting part of the editor's preface to Mrs. Peachey's book. It is a perfect example of the flowery prose of the period:

> "This elegant art requires but the fairy touch of a delicate hand to fill each available space in the chambers or drawing-room with the most perfect and beautiful imitations of the flower garden. Unaffected by change or climate, wax flower modelling perpetuates the transient glories of the floral seasons; places all the tender varieties under the most immediate glance of the ever gratified eye of the artist, who can thus in the depth of winter exhibit to an admiring foreign guest the exotics of the far hemisphere, or the indigenous plants of her own loved land. Who that has watched by the side of an invalid mother, would not feel an exalted pleasure in creating around her the magical representations of those flowerets and rosebuds her maternal hand was wont to rear? Who in such a moment of ministering affection, would not feel how sweet the reward of a father's love, as his approving gaze spoke more than many words his thanks to the duteous child returning the early care of the fond partner of his griefs and joys?"

Who indeed!

8 'DRIZZLING' OR PARFILAGE

It was in the early thirties that I first learned about the curious occupation called 'drizzling'. I was told about it by an old gentleman well on in years, who had had first-hand information from the aunt who had brought him up.

His family had a romantic history, his grandmother having been a 'friend' of the Prince Regent, who had eventually installed her in a well-furnished house in a country town very many miles away from the metropolis. When I knew him my old friend was living surrounded by this furniture, having transferred it all to London.

He told me how the craze for drizzling had spread from France, where it was known as *parfilage*. It was brought over here by the emigrés, who put their knowledge to good use in order to make a few shillings to keep body and soul together.

In the days before the Revolution *parfilage* had been all the rage at the Court of Versailles. It was done quite simply by unravelling brocades, galloons, laces, tassels and braids, etc., in order to extract the gold and silver threads which embellished them. These were then sold to the gold and silversmiths. It was not so much the money, however, which attracted the addicts, but the occupation, which seems to have been both fascinating and compelling. (Unfortunately, many a fine piece of material was completely ruined by this transaction.)

Once the art of *parfilage* was established in this country it immediately became all the rage among the 'bon ton'; again, not so much for the money as for its amusement value.

There was also, I think, another underlying motive which makes the craze seem more reasonable.

For generations it had been thought proper that a woman, however rich or highly born, should not be seen sitting altogether idle; not for fear of 'Satan finding mischief for idle hands', but because the grace and beauty of a woman's hands could be shown off to better advantage when employed with some suitable occupation. The proper movement of hands was an important part of the education of young females, especially in the 18th and early 19th centuries. Girls were taught the proper way to pour out tea and coffee, how to hold a tea-cup and saucer, manipulate a fan, or manage voluminous skirts while curtseying or dancing. Embroidery, netting, tatting and fringe-making were all occupations for making good play with the hands, while the body was in repose and the mind free to indulge in the art of conversation or flirtation. Consequently, when drizzling arrived on the scene it must have been hailed with delight, for the minimum of effort was needed to make a show of being occupied. A little extra pin-money was not to be sneezed at, and there was plenty of material to hand in the now-discarded voluminous brocade dresses of an earlier decade, and in the gold and silver lace which trimmed them – this sort of material was now going rather quickly out of fashion, as plainer materials were needed to achieve the new slim 'Grecian' line. But there was a much quicker and easier source of supply in the gold and silver epaulettes, sabretaches and tassels worn by naval and military officers. These adornments were wheedled from these gentlemen by their female friends and relations to such an extent that apparently an order was made forbidding such traffic in these portions of His Majesty's uniform.

This new occupation was not entirely confined to women. Prince Leopold, widower of Princess Charlotte who had died so tragically in childbirth, took it up, and apparently spent most of his leisure hours in drizzling (though at a time when one would have thought it had gone completely out of fashion). Princess Charlotte may have drizzled after her marriage to him, at any rate she had possessed a tortoiseshell drizzling box, which he used long after she was dead.

In 1828 he induced the young, well-born German actress, Caroline Bauer, to form an alliance with him by promising her a morganatic marriage. This girl of 21 was seventeen years younger than her royal admirer, and trustingly came to England with her mother. They were virtually imprisoned, first in a little house remotely situated in Regent's Park, and afterwards in a gloomy cottage in the grounds of Claremont House, Esher. Leopold had apparently no real intention of marriage – morganatic or otherwise – first it would mean losing the £50,000 a year allowed him by the British Government, and secondly, if he became, as he hoped, King of Greece, he would have to produce a legal and highly-born wife to become his Queen.

But Caroline bore an uncanny resemblance to his dead wife, Charlotte, and for this reason he liked to have her near him; he was, however, by no means the impassioned lover she had expected. He visited her for two hours in the afternoons, and expected her to read aloud to him the novels of the German authoress, Henrietta Hanke, or to play the piano; while he, having produced his tortoiseshell drizzling box, sat and drizzled.

Miss D. A. Ponsonby in her book *A Prisoner in Regent's Park* quotes Caroline as saying to her cousin, Count Christian Stockmar, "I cannot endure it, cousin Christian. I am dying under this deadly love-affair, and of ennui in this golden cage. The Prince never speaks to me of love, never mentions or not he means to marry me. He won't even walk in the garden with me in case someone passing by might recognize him in the company of a young woman! I cannot bear it any longer: the everlasting good Henrietta Hawke, and the mechanical piano playing, while my Amoroso drizzles for ever and ever!"

Occasionally we read about drizzling boxes, but there is some doubt about what they actually look like. Were the boxes big enough to carry the actual piece of material that was being drizzled? Or were they merely boxes to hold the necessary implements? I am inclined to plump for the latter.

Work-bags played such a big part in a woman's equipment according to novels, letters and autobiographies of that time; and a work-bag was a much more accommodating hold-all than a work-box. A work-box big enough to combine both functions was not a common thing. The best examples I can recall were the late 18th- and early 19th-century Sheraton work-boxes made of inlaid mahogany or painted wood with a wooden handle for carrying purposes. The capacious top was domed, and large enough to take any piece of needlework that did not require a frame. In the base was a narrow drawer, not specially fitted, but of sufficient size to hold scissors, bodkins, needles and pins. This would have made a wonderful drizzling box, for few tools were required.

On the other hand, I once bought a beautifully fitted work-box which might have been used in conjunction with a work-bag. It was a hexagonal gold-mounted ivory box fitted with a pair of 'screw-on' pin-cushions, two ivory boxes marked respectively 'Gold' and 'Silver', and a small compartment which could have held scissors and a 'drizzling-pin'. I imagine the work would be pinned on to one or both pin-cushions, and held taut with the left hand, while being drizzled with the right.

Bernard Capes, a much read novelist of the early 20th century, in his novel of the early 19th century *Lake of Wine*, must have known something of this work for one of his characters – Lord Dunlone – employed himself "by ripping the gold thread from a sword knot. For this exquisite had brought his 'Drizzling box' with him – a beautiful tortoiseshell casket, with the Dunlone stock in silver on the lid, and within, a neat array of hilt-bands, shoulder-straps and galloons of tarnished lace – and would sit by the hour together, silent as a trappist, while he unravelled his yarn and wound it upon wooden reels."

One last remark before we leave this fascinating subject. Caroline Bauer states that Prince Leopold had made enough money by his drizzling to buy a silver soup-tureen for his niece Princess Victoria. As the child was only eleven at this time, it seems a singularly inappropriate gift!

BIBLIOGRAPHY

Mrs. Delany at Court and among the Wits. H. BRIMLEY JOHNSON

Small Antique Furniture. B. HUGHES. Lutterworth Press.

Lore and Language of School Children. OPIE. Oxford University Press.

The Romance of Shells. LOUISE ALLARDICE TRAVERS. M. Barrows & Co. Inc., New York.

Hair Embroidery in Siberia and North America. GEOFFREY TURNER. Oxford University Press.

A Prisoner in Regent's Park. D. PONSONBY. Chapman and Hall.

INDEX